D1014618

BEAUTIFUL EYES

ALSO BY PAUL AUSTIN

Something for the Pain:
Compassion and Burnout in the ER

Austin, Paul, 1955-
Beautiful eyes : a
father transformed /
[2014]
33305231551825
ca   12/23/14

BEAUTIFUL

EYES

A Father Transformed

PAUL AUSTIN

W. W. Norton & Company

NEW YORK · LONDON

For Sarah

Copyright © 2014 by Paul Austin

All rights reserved
Printed in the United States of America
First Edition

For information about permission to reproduce selections from this book,
write to Permissions, W. W. Norton & Company, Inc., 500 Fifth Avenue,
New York, NY 10110

For information about special discounts for bulk purchases, please contact
W. W. Norton Special Sales at specialsales@wwnorton.com or 800-233-4830

Manufacturing by Courier Westford
Book design by Kristen Bearse
Production manager: Louise Parasmo

Library of Congress Cataloging-in-Publication Data

Austin, Paul, 1955–
Beautiful eyes : a father transformed / Paul Austin. — First edition.
pages cm
ISBN 978-0-393-08244-9 (hardcover)
1. Austin, Paul, 1955—Health. 2. Down syndrome—Patients—Biography.
3. Father and child. 4. Parents of children with disabilities—Biography.
5. Children with mental disabilities—United States—Biography. I. Title.
RJ506.D68A97 2014
618.92'8588420092—dc23
[B]
2014025600

W. W. Norton & Company, Inc.
500 Fifth Avenue, New York, N.Y. 10110
www.wwnorton.com

W. W. Norton & Company Ltd.
Castle House, 75/76 Wells Street, London W1T 3QT

1 2 3 4 5 6 7 8 9 0

INTRODUCTION

The surgeon held out a gloved hand, palm up, and said, "Scalpel." He made a smooth, long, incision across my wife's belly, below the umbilicus and above the pubic hair. Sally's skin spread. The thin layer of fat glistened yellow, and small red dots appeared along the edges of the skin. One spot blossomed larger, and blood trickled into the incision. The surgical assistant touched the spot with the electrocautery pen, and a blue spark buzzed. A small puff of smoke rose into the cold, bright air, the incense of burned blood.

The latex gloves were smeared with red, but not enough to make them slippery. The exact and silent movements of the surgeon and assistant became more urgent. They dissected and tugged. Gripped and cut. Down through the muscles of the abdominal wall, grasping, stretching, and, digging quickly, down to the hard purple muscle of the uterus. A pause, followed by a low transverse cut, and a gush of clear fluid that sloshed out across the table. The room quieted, save for the slurping sound of the surgeon's hand plunging into the belly, up to the wrist.

The surgeon groped around blindly, found the head, and then pulled upward, wrestling the baby out through the wound.

———

Sally was in bed in the recovery room. I was standing next to her. They had taken the baby somewhere. Dr. Gage pulled the curtain open; the guides in the aluminum track made a clicking, clattering sound. He had taken off his OR hat, and his forehead had a red arc across it. Dark sweat stains were under the arms of his green scrubs.

"I just checked on the baby," he said. "Congratulations. She's beautiful. She seems healthy, had great APGAR scores." He paused. "She has two small heart murmurs—probably a small VSD and a patent ductus."

Sally and I were both medical people, so we understood—two small holes in the heart. A patent ductus is a remnant of fetal circulation: a connection between the aorta and the pulmonary artery, which normally closes at birth. A VSD is a ventriculo-septal defect: a hole in the wall between the two largest chambers of the heart.

I took a deep breath. Maybe it wouldn't be too bad. The VSD could close on its own. So could a patent ductus.

Sally turned her head a few degrees to the side, keeping her eyes on Dr. Gage.

"We'll get an ultrasound of the heart," he said. "Make sure." His voice was gentle and clear.

"And?" Sally said.

"She has Down syndrome."

Sally shrieked. Fists at her side, neck veins bulging, she took a big gasp of air and screamed again. The wailing ricocheted off the walls and ceiling.

My heart beat fast. I leaned down, and placed my forehead next to hers, hairline to hairline.

She continued wailing.

I kept my head touching her head. Her screaming was full throttle.

Her gasps for air became more frequent.

I closed my eyes.

A nurse brought the baby into the recovery room to feed.

"Do you want to hold her?" the nurse said.

I shook my head.

Sally reached out. "Hello, Sarah." Sally's voice was musical, and hoarse from the screaming.

Sally hoisted the bottom edge of her gown and tucked it under her chin. Her breasts were swollen and heavy, with faint blue veins visible through the pale skin. "Let's see how we do."

The nurse watched as Sally grasped her breast.

"Farther back from the nipple," the nurse said. "Sarah needs to get a big mouthful."

Sally held Sarah close, and brushed the baby's cheek against her nipple.

Sarah opened her mouth wide, like she was yawning, and Sally pulled her into her body.

Sally smiled.

"Like a pro," the nurse said.

I let out a pent-up breath.

Sally looked down at Sarah. In oil paintings of the Madonna and child, the light is soft and the shadows softer, and breastfeeding looks peaceful and quiet; it is suffused by a radiant calm. But surrounded by the pastel stripes of this too-bright cubicle, this meeting of saliva and skin, milk and tongue, was a slurping, grunting, air-whistling-through-the-nostrils affair. And there was a cold bright light shining down on this baby.

PART ONE

Chapter One

We had thought we were ready. Sally had been a nurse in labor and delivery, and I was a third-year medical student. This was our first pregnancy, and it had gone well. Neither of us smoked. Sally hadn't drunk any alcohol since we started trying to get pregnant.

She had a dancer's body, and both of us marveled as it changed. From behind, she was still skinny Sally, with her broad shoulders and narrow hips, but when she turned sideways, her belly would swing out into view, massive and majestic, like a full moon filling a horizon.

We were both familiar with the matter-of-fact intimacy of childbirth: the bodily fluids and animal smells, the laboring woman's face red, her eyes squinched tight, legs spread wide, the baby slithering out fast like an otter, so sleek, the legs trailing, umbilical cord corkscrewing, glistening, it all happening so fast after all those hours of labor.

We had both scrubbed in on C-sections as well, and knew the measured cadence of the surgeon's work. Every move choreographed, practiced, and precise. It begins slowly but the pace picks up as they cut through the layers of the belly, down to the baby, and pull it up, out into the light and air.

We had both read *What to Expect When You're Expecting*.

———

A month earlier, Sally and I were in our apartment at married student housing, lying on our backs, touching hip and shoulder. "There are three of us in this bed," Sally whispered, slowly skimming her hand across her bare belly. She turned toward me, and brushed the hair from her face. "Yow," she said. "Somebody's stretching." She took my hand and placed it against her belly. "Feel that? Must be a foot."

The skin of her abdomen was smooth and warm, and stretched tight. The uterus, firm beneath her skin, felt muscular. A solid little lump pressed up against my palm. For weeks, Sally had been feeling the baby move—she would grab my hand and put it against her belly so I could feel it too. But I was always a fraction of a second too late.

Years before, lying on our backs beneath a late summer sky, long after midnight—Sally's idea—we were watching for shooting stars. "There's one," she said, pointing off to our left. I missed it. I gazed again, straight up. "Another one," she said. "And another."

Finally I saw one, a silent white streak, impossibly thin against the black and star-crowded sky.

I felt the baby's movement just a second too late. Too slow. And a fear that perhaps I was missing it because I was trying too hard. Wanting it too much.

"What's it feel like?" I asked.

Sally looked down and placed her hands on her belly. "When I first felt it, it was like a butterfly inside, opening and closing its wings. Now it feels stretchy."

The smells of our bed—so familiar and subtle that I hardly noticed them—seemed richer. And the way I nuzzled Sally's neck was different. Gratitude was involved, and mystery. And at the center of the mystery was the way her body was changing.

We were playful as we accommodated the expanding heft of her belly. Our bodies moved with a rhythm that needed no instruction: like breathing or swallowing, every cell moved exactly as it should. And each cell was packed with a wispy double helix of DNA, those angstrom-thin strands that coded for our humanity and tethered us to our ancestral past.

We'd been married three years when Sally got pregnant. We hadn't done amniocentesis because, based on the results of the preliminary tests—blood drawn from a vein in Sally's arm—the risk of accidentally causing a miscarriage of a normal child was greater than the likelihood of discovering a chromosomal abnormality. The doctor's face had been kind, and his words were softly spoken, but the phrases he used, "normal child" and "chromosomal abnormality," carried an unspoken assumption with which I became complicit: that some people are "normal,"* and others are not.

---

* The term "normal," when used to distinguish persons without disabilities from those with disabilities, is at its core offensive. It is, however, a word I have used, and to pretend otherwise would be untrue. Later in this book I'll talk about the way this nomenclature distorts the way we think about one another.

Chapter Two

Dr. Gage, the obstetrician, came to talk with us again in the post-op bay.

"Have you chosen a name?" His tone was pleasant, matter-of-fact.

We'd been planning to name the baby Sarah if it was a girl. But I didn't know if we wanted to still use that name. We'd been expecting a different child. A normal one. I looked at Sally.

"Sarah," she said. "We'll call her Sarah." Sally's voice was raspy.

"What a pretty name," Dr. Gage said, "and what a pretty baby."

Sally and I stared at him.

"Sarah will be more like other children," he said, "than unlike them." He paused, and then said, "The pediatricians will want a chromosomal analysis, but that's just a formality." He looked to Sally, and then me. "She has it."

Sally's lips tightened. Her eyes squinted against the glare of the light above.

"We'll get an echo of Sarah's heart. She may or may not need surgery." He paused again.

Maybe the hole in her heart would be so big she wouldn't survive. She could die on the OR table. We could put her in a small white coffin, deal with the loss, and then move on. Try again in a couple of years. Have a normal family. I felt my face flush.

"Sometimes a parent feels that it may be best if a child dies painlessly and quickly." He looked from me to Sally, and back to me. "Others don't have that feeling. Whatever you're feeling, you should know that lots of people have felt the same way."

I felt like crying. I took a deep breath and felt my lungs expand. I let it out, slowly.

"For the first few months," Dr. Gage said, "you'll be caught up in all the routine baby stuff: breastfeeding, diapers, car seats, and baby buggies. But in about six months you'll get the hang of it, and then all of the other issues will bubble up. A new baby puts a huge stress on a marriage. I tell all couples to think about seeing a counselor at about six months. Just to air things out. For you guys, I think it would be especially important."

I nodded along with Sally, but I was faking it. *Six months? I don't know how we'll make it to tomorrow morning.*

"One last thing," Dr. Gage said. "This isn't your fault.

When something like this happens, we always look for a reason—it's human nature to want to know what could've caused it, or some way it could've been avoided. But in this case it's nothing you ate, drank, or smoked. Nothing you did or didn't do. It just happened."

I felt my lower lip tremble, and tears begin to form. I finally knew what I was feeling. Stricken. If I looked at Sally, I would be overwhelmed. I stared down at the puckered blue booties still covering my shoes.

"When you get unexpected news," Dr. Gage said, "it's impossible to remember everything, so I'm going to ask you to remember just three basic things."

Sally and I both looked at his face.

"Sarah will be more like other children than not." He held up his thumb. "You should get some help in six months." He held up his index finger. "And it isn't anything you did or didn't do—it just happened." He extended his middle finger. "Okay?"

I looked at Dr. Gage and nodded. From the corner of my eye, I saw Sally nod too.

"Can you say it back to me?" Dr. Gage asked. He was looking at me.

My mind was blank.

"Sarah will be like other children," Dr. Gage said. "You may want to see a counselor in six months, and it isn't anything you did or didn't do." His face was so earnest. He wanted so much to ease our pain.

"She'll be like other children." My voice sounded raspy. "We should see a marriage counselor." I cleared my throat. "And it isn't our fault." I believed the first two things.

Chapter Three

Sally lay motionless in the hospital bed. Asleep. The night-light's amber glow kept me company in the dark as I dozed, woke up, shifted in my chair, and nodded off again. Each time I woke, there was a moment of hope that none of this had happened, and that I was at our apartment, and that Sally was beside me, still pregnant. But the side rails of Sally's hospital bed, and the quiet murmur of the nurses' station across the hall, brought me back to this chair. This room.

Sally's hair fanned out against the pillow. Her breathing was quiet and regular. Sarah was in a bassinet in the newborn nursery. I'd held her earlier, so tiny, almost weightless in my arms. I'd been relieved to hand her back to Sally. I stood and stretched, and looked out of the window again. The sky was still black—the stars washed out by the mercury lights above the empty parking lot adjacent to the hospital. Doctors' parking. Across Manning Drive, cars came and went from the parking deck, all night. Family members. I sat back in the recliner, and closed my eyes again.

Anne-Marie, an intern, knocked quietly on the door and tip-toed into the room. I must have dozed off again. I checked my watch. Five forty-five. Anne-Marie was pre-rounding: checking on her patients before morning rounds, during which she would update the attending—the doctor in charge—on each patient's status. A couple of months earlier, during my rotation on obstetrics, I had been assigned to her team.

"Good morning," Anne-Marie whispered, as if hoping to check on us without waking us completely. I appreciated her thoughtfulness: when the other intern on the team entered, he would snap on the lights and bellow out, "Congratulations. How's my favorite mother and baby doing on this beautiful morning?" The couple—if the father was present—would startle and blink.

"I like to find out if everyone is okay before I say too much," Anne-Marie had told me, late one night, on the labor and delivery ward. "It's easy to assume that people are happy about a new baby. But you never know."

Anne-Marie used her penlight to check the bandage across Sally's lower belly, from the C-section. She pulled on a pair of exam gloves and gently prodded the white silk tape. "Clean, dry, and intact," she whispered. She knew that Sally was a nurse and knew what to look for on the bandages after surgery. "I need to check your lochia," she said. Lochia is the postpartum vaginal discharge—blood, mucus, bits of placenta. Anne-Marie hooked a finger under the elastic band that held Sally's menstrual pad, pulled it forward, and shined her penlight onto Sally's crotch. "Good down here, too," she said, as she pulled the covers back up to Sally's waist. "Breasts okay?"

"Just a little sore," Sally whispered back. "Not bad."

"Good," Anne-Marie said. "See you again in an hour or so." She turned to me. "You okay, Paul?"

"I'm fine," I whispered back.

———

At seven o'clock, Anne-Marie and Dr. Gage came by. The rest of the team—medical students, interns, third- and fourth-year residents—all stayed in the hallway, instead of herding into the room as they normally would. I didn't know if this was because I was a student here, or if it was because our baby had Down syndrome. Either way, it was fine with me. I really didn't want to see anyone unless I had to.

———

Sally had breakfast, and dozed in the hospital bed. I was in the vinyl-covered recliner, my back to the window. The morning sun was warm on my right shoulder. The cushions of the chair sagged: I was not the first new father to sit in this chair.

Probably not the first one to feel trapped, either. But Sally and I were better off than a lot of new parents. During the second year of medical school, in genetics class, I had learned about an entire universe of human maldevelopment. Our textbook was filled with black and white photographs of malformed humans: page after page of disconjugate gazes, pigeon chests, and extra digits. Dwarves holding hands, acromegalics with bulging foreheads and protuberant jaws.

The dispassionate tone of the textbook didn't erase the feeling of a carnival freak show. Some pictures looked like mug shots: one view facing forward and one from the side. Others were full-frontal photographs: breasts with small dark nipples, thick thatches of pubic hair, small phallic nubbins shrunken from cold or fear, arms to the side with palms turned forward, eyes staring straight into the camera. These were subjects. They were specimens. Some of the eyes were covered with a black stripe, to protect the individual's privacy. I was never sure whose shame those stripes were meant to assuage: the person in the picture, or the person staring at it.

The most photogenic children were the ones with Down

syndrome. Those smiling faces seemed less scary, more approachable than the others. Guileless. But when I read the printed text beneath the photographs, I was stunned by the list of dysmorphic features. Epicanthal folds—a downward tuck of skin at the corner of the eyes that give a slanted appearance. Brushfield spots in the iris—small white specks in the pigment's periphery, focal aggregations of connective tissue. A small nose with a flat bridge. Small, low-set ears. Flattening of the back of the skull. A tendency of the tongue to protrude. A single crease in the palm of the hand. A wide space between the big toe and the second. Depression. Alzheimer's. Heart defects.

I shifted in my chair. Sarah had two heart problems: a VSD—ventriculo-septal defect, which is a hole in the wall between the two lower chambers of the heart—and a patent ductus—a remnant of the fetal circulatory system. She'd had the cardiac ultrasound; the defects were small and wouldn't need surgery.

I looked at Sally. Her eyes were closed and her respirations easy. Sleeping or resting; either way, she was closed down.

Sunk back into the comfort of the vinyl chair, my body was tired, but I was wide awake. There was no way out.

My eyes felt tired. I closed them. The August sun felt good on my shoulder, but the room was air-conditioned to the point of being chilly. I could go to the nurses' station and ask to have the AC turned down, or ask for a blanket. Probably could get a warm one. But I might see a classmate and have to answer questions about Sarah.

I settled back into the forgiving, cushioned chair, and felt myself drift toward sleep.

I woke with a start, and looked around the room. Sally's eyes were open. I'd drooled in my sleep. I wiped my chin with my palm, and then wiped it against my jeans, and wiped my face again. "Reminds me of studying in the library at UNC," I whispered, unsure of why I was whispering since it was daylight outside. "Surest way to have a good-looking woman sit nearby—doze off and wake up with your face covered in drool."

Sally smiled, but her eyes didn't crinkle.

"We okay?" I asked.

She shook her head. It looked as if she were saying she wasn't sure. She might have been saying no.

"Oh, Paul, you're going to learn so much." Elaine was one of our first visitors. Her hands were clasped together and she leaned forward, her forehead creased, eyebrows raised at the center, sloping downward. "You're going to learn about patience, and acceptance, and unconditional love." Her eyes were light blue, and sharply focused on mine. A small meniscus of tears formed in each lower lid.

I felt myself leaning away from her.

"You didn't know, did you?" Elaine touched my arm. "My Tony. He has Down syndrome." She looked over at Sally, sitting in the bed. "He's twelve."

Elaine and I had worked together in the ER when I was a nursing assistant paying for college. A fit woman about my age, she always wore a white turtleneck, dark blue scrub pants with an elastic waistband, and a light blue jacket. She'd sometimes laugh along with us at the cynical jokes in the nurses' station. She was a competent nurse, but never the first to grab a dying patient's arm and start poking with an IV. She was more likely to be one row back, documenting the code as it went along, or going to get the crash cart, or calling X-Ray to say we needed a STAT portable chest x-ray. She lacked that hard little edge that seems useful in an emergency, as if she was too emotionally porous, or too aware of how high the stakes were, to be the one the docs called out for when a patient was dying.

"It gets better," she continued. "Easier."

"Thanks," Sally said. Her voice was still hoarse from the day before.

"Is the baby all right?" Elaine asked. "Otherwise?"

"Small VSD," I said. "And a patent ductus. Neither needs to be fixed."

"Good." Her tone was emphatic, and her ponytail bounced as she nodded. "Tony needed open-heart. He did great, but I'm glad your kiddo won't need it. Boy or girl?"

"Girl," Sally said. "Sarah."

A nurse I hadn't seen before stood in the doorway, holding our daughter. "Knock knock," she said.

I twisted in my chair to see her. "Come in."

"Someone's hungry," the nurse said. She jostled Sarah gently.

"May I?" Elaine stood, and pulled open the corner of the receiving blanket. "She's beautiful."

Sally smiled. I did too. Reflex. Our daughter wasn't beautiful, and I knew it. But I liked Elaine and appreciated her effort to help us. And I was quickly learning to pretend. I had missed my chance to be a proud new father. But I could fake it.

"I won't intrude any longer," Elaine said. She handed Sally a scrap of paper. "My name and number. Call any time. Any reason."

"Thanks." Sally's eyes filled with tears. "I will."

Elaine turned to me, holding her arms out for a hug.

"You take care of yourself," she said. The force of her embrace surprised me.

———

Sally pulled down a small triangular flap on her nursing bra. Her breasts were swollen and hard.

"Engorged?" the nurse asked.

"Maybe a little." Sally prodded her breast with two fingers. "Sore."

"This'll help." She handed Sarah to Sally.

Sally caught her lower lip between her teeth as she guided Sarah's mouth to her nipple. Sally relaxed back against the pillows.

When Sarah was done, Sally placed her against her shoulder and burped her.

I rewrapped her in the flannel receiving blanket, and held her in my lap.

Someone had sent us a flower arrangement—pink carnations and roses, surrounded by baby's breath. I pulled a small carnation free and broke off the stem, and slipped the flower behind Sarah's left ear as she slept. Sally smiled. Her eyes crinkled, for the first time in two days.

I looked back to the flower beside Sarah's downward-slanting eyes. I felt my face flush hot, paralyzed by the simple fact of a newborn and a flower.

Later, when the nurse came to take Sarah back to the nursery, she laughed and silently clapped her hands when she saw our daughter snuffling in her sleep. "Look at you," she said. "The prettiest girl at the party."

I was relieved that the flower looked playful. It's how I had meant it: playful and hopeful. My daughter didn't belong in a black and white photograph with a black stripe across her face in some textbook. See? She has a pink carnation behind her ear.

Chapter Four

Sarah was down the hall in the newborn nursery. Three days old. She was probably lying in her bassinet, her face revealing none of the mysteries of her sleep. Perhaps in her dreams she heard the proximate thump of her mother's heart, and felt the transmitted vibration of blood pulsing through Sally's aorta, that muscular artery that courses like a garden hose down the center of the body.

Maybe Sarah was dreaming of the steady rhythmic swoosh of maternal venous blood flowing back from Sally's legs and up the vena cava—a soft sound, like surf rolling in and receding heard from a protected spot among the dunes. Perhaps Sarah was recalling the uterine warmth of salty water. Maybe she would flinch in her sleep, reliving in her dreams that startling first breath of cold, dry air rushing down her windpipe and into her lungs, after months of the warm brine of amniotic fluid—the only atmosphere she'd known. Maybe Sarah dreamed of the new and nubby feel of Sally's nipple against her tongue. The sweet taste of milk.

Sally and I were in her hospital room. She was awake, but her eyes were closed. Resting.

Slumped in the vinyl chair, I listened to the murmured conversation drift across the hall from the nurses' station. A new mother's slippers made a raspy whisper as she shuffled up and down the hallway. Her baby was probably normal.

On the first day of Sarah's life, the nurses took some of her blood to do a karyotype—a process that results in a photograph of all of her chromosomes—that would confirm the diagnosis of Down syndrome. I'd seen pictures of chromosomes in the biology textbook in college and, of course, in the genetics books in medical school: the chromosomes matched up two by two, like sets of twin caterpillars or sea worms, with bandings of black, white, and faded shades of gray. Forty-six chromosomes: twenty-three pairs, lined up, tallest on the left, shortest on the right. The number of human chromosomes, forty-six, is now an accepted fact: as obvious as our two eyes and ten toes.

But for years, scientists didn't know the actual number.[1] Some thought we had sixteen chromosomes, others forty-nine. Eventually, the scientific community came to the incorrect consensus of forty-eight.[2] For the next forty years, researcher after researcher peered into a microscope and, using the camera lucida technique, made tracings of what they saw. Then they carefully counted, and consistently came up with forty-eight. It's easy to understand. The reproductions of early karyotypes look like Rorschach prints of garden snails clustered around a salt trap.

In 1955, a scientist named Joe Hin Tjio made a preparation that was countable; he used colchicine to stop the cells in mitosis, thereby "catching" the chromosomes in their condensed form. Tjio also gently compressed the cells with a slight tap on the thin coverglass to free the cytoplasm from the cell membrane, and another tap to flatten out the chromosomes. I imagine the scientist gently tapping the paper-thin glass of the slide cover like a kid rapping on the glass of an aquarium, or a new dad tapping on the glass of the newborn nursery.

Tjio used hypotonic solutions to spread the chromosomes out, making them easier to see, and count. He studied cells in tissue culture, a set of techniques that allow cells to be grown in a broth. Tjio studied fetal lung fibroblasts, which grow quickly, dividing often.[3]

Tjio was able to get the chromosomes to scatter without overlap, so they could be counted. Forty-six. An accomplished photographer,[4] he sent photomicrographs to friends and scientists with a small, typed note in the lower left corner: "Human cell with 46 chromosomes observed 1955 on December 22nd at 2:00 am." I wonder at the quiet pride he must have felt in those after-midnight hours as he typed out the time, and date, when we could finally count, without equivocation, the chromosomes—those "colored bodies"—that code our very existence.

———

Four years later, in January of 1959, Jérôme Lejeune, along with Marthe Gautier and Raymond Turpin, published a scientific paper about children with Down syndrome, in which they described the presence of three copies, instead of two, of chromosome number twenty-one.[5] It was a major scientific breakthrough.

Lejeune, a recent graduate of the Paris School of Medicine, had been put in charge of a group of children who, at that time, were still called "mongolian idiots" or "mongols" by the medical community—based on the prevailing medical theory left over from Victorian times, that these children resulted from an intrauterine reversion to an earlier, less advanced racial strain. This theory had been put forth by John Langdon Down in 1866, after he read Darwin's recently published work on natural selection.

Lejeune rejected the intrauterine reversion theory. In the course of his work as a pediatrician—white coat, stethoscope, and tongue depressors—Lejeune had noted that the mongolian idiots from Mongolia looked more like mongolian idiots from England than they did their own Mongolian parents. So the intrauterine reversion theory couldn't be right. Lejeune reasoned that it must have to do with a hereditary mechanism.

The Second World War had ended just a few years previously, and in the austerity of postwar France it was difficult to get access to lab equipment. Lejeune began to study the handprints of children with Down syndrome, because they have just one crease running diagonally across the palm, rather than the normal three. This is something our obstetrician had noticed about Sarah. This single crease was named the "simian crease," because apes have just one palmar crease. The course that the single line follows across the palm varies between the different species of ape; a monkey's is different from a chimp's. Lejeune and his mentor, Raymond Turpin, hypothesized that these differences in the palmar crease of apes must have resulted from many, many single-gene changes, transmitted over the centuries of evolutionary time. The distinctive pattern in the palms of children with Down syndrome, they further reasoned, must be the result of a change in multiple genes transmitted all at the same time. For this to happen, all of those genes would have to be on the same chromosome.[6]

In 1957, Marthe Gautier, a physician who had recently

learned tissue culture during a year abroad in Boston, returned to Paris and began to work under the direction of Dr. Turpin. With his approval, she began to grow cells that could be examined using modifications of the techniques developed by Tjio and other successful cytologists. Using a microscope discarded by the hospital's microbiology department—the focusing gears were so worn that Lejeune had to slip a piece of tinfoil from a cigarette wrapper between them to stabilize them—Lejeune and Gautier began to examine the chromosomes of people with Down syndrome. They noticed a triple copy of chromosome 21.

Lejeune and his coworkers published "Étude des Chromosomes Somatiques de Neuf Enfants Mongoliens" ("Study of the Somatic Chromosomes of Nine Mongoloid Children"). The paper was barely two pages long, but it changed medical history: it was the first time that scientists could link a specific disease to a specific chromosomal abnormality.

A couple of years later, Lejeune and eighteen other scientists published a letter to the editor of *Lancet*, one of the world's most prestigious medical journals: "It has long been recognized," the scientists wrote, "that the terms 'mongolian idiocy,' 'mongolism,' 'mongoloid,' etc. as applied to a specific type of mental deficiency, have misleading connotations."[7] The authors spent a few lines describing the problems with the nomenclature and concluded: "We urge, therefore, that the expressions which imply a racial aspect of the condition no longer be used." As alternatives they suggested "Langdon Down anomaly," "Down's syndrome or anomaly," and "trisomy 21 anomaly." The letter closed with: "It is hoped that agreement on a specific phrase will soon crystallize once the term 'mongolism' has been abandoned."

Lejeune went on to write over 500 published papers, identifying multiple chromosomal abnormalities. A gregarious man, he rode a bicycle to work and whittled rosaries to give as gifts. He was a close advisor to Pope John Paul II.[8] As a Catholic and as a scientist, Lejeune believed that an egg and a sperm combined to form a unique human life—a fully human life; he publicly and passionately opposed abortion. His outspoken stance was widely thought to have cost him the Nobel Prize for his work in cytogenetics and his other scientific interest, the dangers of atomic radiation exposure.[9]

In the biography of Lejeune by his daughter, there's a photograph of him, a handsome man with a thick thatch of white hair and a trim white mustache, wearing a dark suit, a dark tie, and a white shirt. Two children with Down syndrome sit on his lap, and two teenagers with Down syndrome stand behind him. The caption reads, "Jérôme Lejeune with his 'dear little ones.'"

On first glance, the term "dear little ones" seems saccharine to me. Condescending, facile, and unearned. But then I imagine a young doctor fresh out of medical school, returning from his stint in the military to take over the care of a clinic full of children who were still called "mongolian idiots." Was this the prize he had been working toward: caring for children whose hands had "simian creases"? I wondered what prompted him to study something as humble as their handprints: the most basic assertion of self, like the prehistoric hands traced between the bison, horses, and deer in the caves of Lascaux, or the small wet prints on the fogged windows of a school bus.

From the creases and whorls of handprints, Lejeune turned his attention to chromosomes—the most condensed little packet of "self" that exists. He cared enough about these children to make them his life's work. And he was among the first to stand up and say that it was time to quit calling them "mongolian idiots."

So, if Lejeune wanted to call children with Down syndrome "my dear little ones," who was I to find fault with the sweet words he used to describe them?

———

In June of 2007, a course of canonization was begun in the Roman Catholic Church. There was a compelling case for sainthood: a loving husband and father, Lejeune had devoted his entire career to a group of marginalized people, and as a devout Catholic, he had been a staunch opponent of abortion. As the world-renowned scientist who had discovered trisomy 21, he had opposed prenatal testing.

But in 2009, Marthe Gautier published a different narrative.[10] By her account, Lejeune, a protégé of Dr. Turpin, had shown only passing interest in cell culture and chromosomal analysis until after she produced microscopic slides that clearly showed the chromosomes.

As part of her medical training, Dr. Gautier had spent a year in the United States, studying pediatric heart disease. While in the States, she'd also been given a second job, as a technician in a cell culture lab. When she returned to Paris, she was assigned to work under Dr. Turpin, a pediatric research director she had never met. The French medical research culture of the time was very hierarchical, and was not welcoming to women (in 1950, out of eighty interns, only two were women).[11]

In early 1956, after attending the International Human Genetics Conference, at which it was announced that there were definitely forty-six, not forty-eight, human chromosomes, Dr. Turpin lamented aloud that there was no lab in Paris that could examine the chromosomes of mongoloids. Since she'd recently been doing tissue culture in the States, young Dr. Gautier offered "to do what I could do," if given lab space.[12]

A vacant lab was found, "with a refrigerator, a centrifuge, an empty cupboard, and a low-definition microscope." Dr. Gautier started her lab from scratch, taking out a personal loan to buy flasks, pipettes, test tubes, and a distilled water apparatus. She bought a rooster for plasma. For human plasma, she used her own; this was, she said, "an economical and reliable procedure."

Her scientific technique was stringent: she didn't use antibiotics or colchicine in her preparations, and did not do subcultures after trypsin treatment, for fear of inducing chromosomal changes that would confound her results. She adapted the techniques of Tjio, but instead of hypotonic medium she used isotonic serum, to keep the membranes intact. She never "squashed" the cells, as had been recommended by Tjio and others, and allowed them to dry on a microscope slide before staining them. "Thus," she said, "my best preparations were in prometaphase, without cell membrane breakage, and so produced an exact figure and beautiful elongated chromosomes, easy to pair and unbroken. These results were not accomplished until after a few failures."

Jérôme Lejeune, a protégé of Dr. Turpin, began to stop by the lab. Tissue from mongol children was obtained, and Gautier was able to produce a slide that showed, unmistakably, that those cells had forty-seven chromosomes, not forty-six. "My gamble, which was that I would succeed alone with my laboratory workers at my technique and above all discover an anomaly, had paid off. It is a French discovery, something that was not apparent at the start."

Dr. Gautier continued, "The additional chromosome was small, and the laboratory did not have a photomicroscope that would confirm its presence and establish the karyotype. I entrusted the slides to J.L., who had the photos taken but did not show them to me; they were, he said, with the Chief and therefore under lock and key."

Without telling Dr. Gautier or Dr. Turpin, Dr. Lejeune announced at a scientific meeting in Canada that he had discovered a third copy of chromosome 21.

Other labs around the world had also been making slides of chromosomes, racing to be the first to discover a chromosomal cause of a disease. Lejeune hastily presented the results to the Academy of Sciences in France because the proceedings would be published within three days, instead of having a two-month delay, as was the case for most international publications.

Throughout the research community, the first name to appear on a paper is always the name of the scientist who has done the majority of the work, and the last name is the person who supervised the lab. If Gautier's version of history is correct, her name should have been first. But when the paper came out, the names appeared as Lejeune, Gautier, and Turpin.

By Dr. Gautier's account, Lejeune had grabbed her slides and claimed credit for her work.

"Progressively," Dr. Gautier wrote fifty years later, "through his participation in numerous congresses, he [Lejeune] was hailed as the only discoverer and ended up convincing himself of that, to such an extent that Professor Turpin's descendants kicked up a fuss through their lawyers. In addition, they lodged in the Pasteur Institute's archives their father's articles certifying his seniority in the chromosome-based hypothesis concerning mongolism, which was finally verified."

Should Lejeune be canonized as a saint or cursed as a thief? Until I read Gautier's account, I liked him. And who wouldn't? He was a scientist who rode a bicycle to work and dedicated his professional life to disabled children. He put his principles above a Nobel Prize. Yet I tended to believe Gautier. Had a moment of unbridled ambition prompted Lejeune to swoop in and snatch Gautier's slides? Or had Turpin encouraged him to take the credit, because it would be unseemly for a woman to make such an important scientific breakthrough? It is unclear if we will ever know: Turpin died in 1988, and Lejeune died in 1994.

Our obstetrician had said that Sarah's karyotype would take at least a couple of days. That was okay with Sally and me. We were in no hurry to confirm the diagnosis. There had never been any real doubt.

Sally and I were in no hurry to do anything, really. We needed a few days filled with daily events: a nurse bringing Sarah in to breastfeed, and the ladies from dietary bringing up bulky fiberglass trays of half-warm food. "It's good," Sally said. Her voice still had a faint husky burr.

The meat on Sally's tray was uniform and monochromatic, half an inch thick, and covered with gray-brown gravy. She was given Jell-o. A fruit cup. Sally poked the Jell-o with her spoon and grinned. "Jiggly." She had always denied any feeling of displeasure or anger. She smiled when she was happy, and she smiled when she was mad. It was the way she was raised.

She planned to stay in the hospital for as long as they'd let her. The standard stay after a C-section was four days. Sally was holding out for five. She wanted to hibernate as long as she could. Eat the meat. Poke the Jell-o. Smile.

Part of me wanted to get away from the hospital—at any time a classmate might drop in and I'd have to smile and show them my daughter, exposing myself and the flawed child I'd engendered. But another part of me wanted to forget the outside world, burrow into that chair, and hide forever.

The chair's vinyl covering had a leatherlike texture stamped into its surface, except where it had been worn smooth and shiny. My fingertips rested on a smooth spot, and gently smoothed it further. How had this happened? In college and medical school I'd learned the facts of it, memorizing every step in the dance of cell division. Made note cards, colored pencils scattered across the kitchen table, lightly sketching in the cellular structures with a number two pencil, inking it in with a black extra-fine felt-tip, blowing on the card to make the ink dry faster, and then erasing the stray pencil marks with an art gum eraser, leaving the black ink stark and bold on the bright white index card. By drawing the cells, I began to under-stand the words and pictures I'd been trying to memorize. Cell membranes, the nuclear envelope, Golgi apparatus, mitochondria. Chromosomes.

As I drew the tiny structures and began to believe in their physicality, I started to understand how the microscopic components all worked together, like a bicycle derailleur, or the dusty drum brakes of my MG, or the ligaments of a knee joint. I enjoyed drawing the wispy strings of DNA—the double helix looks like a ladder with twisted rails—long strings of adenine, guanine, cytosine, and thymine, paired up between the endless corkscrews of the sugar-phosphate side rails.

My note cards were covered with stick-figure pictures of the molecules. I felt like a scientist chalking structures onto a slate chalkboard: the five-sided ring of the sugar molecules, the six-sided rings of carbon and nitrogen, all of those molecules with so much more space than structure. I didn't think I'd ever use the information as a doctor—I wanted to be a surgeon, or an ER doctor, work with my hands. I'd never specialize in genetics or do scientific research. I admired doctors like Gautier and Langdon Down, but I wasn't one of them.

But still, I enjoyed making the drawings of DNA. More emptiness than line: two long, skinny chains of molecules, each going in opposite directions, pairing up like two sides of a zipper, and then twisted like a coil of pasta.

When it's time to make new molecules of DNA, the two strings unzip by means of an enzyme that moves along like a tiny Zamboni that gnashes, clicks, and hums, all switches and levers, clicks and ratcheting sounds, unzipping the two strands, so that other enzymes can scurry along the unzipped single strands, linking up the molecules, adenine with thymine, guanine with cytosine, more clicking and humming, until eventually there are two identical double strands, each a mirror to the other. I loved the drawings on my note cards and my growing understanding of how life recreated itself, down to the level of the cell. The molecule. Such precision. Elegance.

Why hadn't it worked for Sarah?

———

The day before we were supposed to go home, Dr. Gage, our obstetrician, told us that the karyotype was done, and that it confirmed Down syndrome. Sally and I nodded, both of us keeping our eyes on Dr. Gage. Sarah was asleep in her plexiglass bassinet. "The geneticist would be glad to talk with you," Dr. Gage said.

Sally wasn't ready to meet with the geneticist. She told me to go ahead if I wanted to.

Dr. Anderson's office was small, with books jammed together on shelves and stacked on the floor. She pushed photocopies of research papers back and forth on her desk until there was a clear space, and carefully placed a card the size of a typewriter paper in front of me. It was heavy stock, ivory in color.

I held the edges of the card as if it were a photograph I didn't want to smudge. It was preprinted with a heading, "CYTOGENETICS LABORATORY, CHROMOSOME

ANALYSIS," with spaces for patient identification. Someone had carefully filled in the information with a black
felt-tip pen:

NAME: AUSTIN BABY

LAB NO: B3971BA

CELL NO: 8

CHROMOSOME DX: 'B' 47 XX + 21

The rest of the card was printed with spaces for each
of the twenty-three sets of chromosomes. The spaces
were labeled 1–22 for the autosomes, and then there was
one more space off to the side for the allosomes—the sex
chromosomes—XX or XY. Each individual chromosome
had been cut out by hand, the scissor marks evident: some
of the curves had been made with long, smooth, gradual
cuts, others looked as if they'd been snipped in short nib-
bling cuts, leaving tiny angular tangents. Unlike the karyotypes in books, which showed the best examples from
research labs, my daughter's chromosomes all had distinctive shapes: snaky curves, shepherd's crooks, hockey sticks,
one that looked like a capital C, another like an F without
its crossbar.

The chromosomes were lined up in descending size, from
the tall, lanky marathon runner-shaped chromosome 1 to
the small and chunky chromosome 23. And right there, on

the short line labeled 21, were three little nubbins, a triplet of ovoids pasted carefully in place.

I turned the card over, trying to feel the link between these chromosomes lined up on heavy card stock and the way my daughter looked. On the other side was a tear-shaped glossy photograph of the slide from which they'd cut the chromosomes, which were scattered randomly on a background of mottled gray. They were spread out like tea leaves, or casting runes, or a handful of worms tossed on the ground after a slow day of fishing. Seen this way—captured as they'd fallen, rather than all lined up—they looked even more like prehistoric organic things: bacteria, or microtubules of some sort, tiny sea creatures inching along the floor of the ocean.

I turned the card back over and saw them all paired up. Number 21, the next to last, the car before the caboose, still had three little chromosomes.

I felt as if I was holding something that was already becoming an artifact, like Sarah's birth certificate—the "Certificate of Delivery." It was of the same heavy card stock as the karyotype but it looked like a diploma, with preprinted Gothic lettering.

Sarah's name, all capital letters, had been typed in on an IBM Selectric; the date, August 26, 1987. The card had been rolled into the typewriter at a subtle slant and the typing all sloped upward, the bottoms of the letters and numbers just below the line. Below that, Sarah's weight: 6 lbs, 15 oz. And then the parents' names: Paul Ethan Austin and Sally Rish Somers.

The certificate had been pressed with Sarah's footprints, each one wide at the front, narrow at the heel, the skin criss-crossed with wrinkles, the five small dots of toes. The prints are as specific as the nameband—a clear, soft plastic sleeve, Sarah's name typed on a slip of paper tucked inside, the brace-let secured with the plastic button the nurse snapped together with a soft clicking sound around Sarah's ankle, which was no larger than two fingers held together side to side.

These lined-up chromosomes and typed-out names were how we would identify our child: know who she was, who she could become. And once the ink and glue had dried, it couldn't be changed. It could be destroyed or burned, refuted or denied. But never changed.

I registered, again, the careful homemade aspect of the cutouts. A person, not a machine, had put together this karyotype, this collage of snapshots.

"How do you do this?" I held up the card and looked at Dr. Anderson, the cytogeneticist.

"We start with a sample of blood." Her voice was matter-of-fact. "Peripheral blood. Then we culture up the T-cells. Suspension culture."

I had worked in a research lab the summer before. I could picture the clear plastic, rectangular flasks with orange caps, labeled and stacked, each one with a quarter-inch of pink liquid layered across the bottom. We had to use sterile technique, to keep bacteria from growing.

"After twenty-four to forty-eight hours," Dr. Anderson said, "we add colchicine to arrest the cells in metaphase. It also makes the chromosomes condense."

"Metaphase" is Greek for "between stages," a brief moment during cell division in which the chromosomes have been duplicated and are all paired off and lined up at the equator, ready to be pulled apart into two daughter cells.

"Then we spin it down to a soft pellet, wash it, spin it, wash it, and then dilute it out with hypotonic potassium chloride. Everything is done slowly, in a droplike fashion, to keep from disrupting the cells."

"How big is the pellet?" I asked.

She picked up a stub of a pencil, half its eraser gone. "About this big," she said, placing her thumb midway down what was left of the eraser. "If it's from an amniocentesis, there can be so few cells you're not even sure you've got a pellet." She held her hand up, as if holding a small test tube between her thumb and forefinger, and squinted. "But with peripheral blood samples, it's pretty big.

"Then we give it one last spin and put a couple of drops

on a cold wet slide. Then we warm it, dry it, and check with a phase contrast scope to see if we've got what we think we've got. If we do, we then stain it with G stain, to show the banding. Then we take a picture, develop the film, and make the prints."

"In a darkroom? Like photographers use?"

She nodded. "Then we use scissors. Like these." Dr. Anderson pulled a pair of small silver scissors from her pencil holder. They looked like embroidery scissors. "On Fridays, the clinics want the results before they go home, and we're in here, chromosomes everywhere. Don't sneeze."

We both chuckled.

Dr. Anderson and I knew each other from the genetics class she'd taught in medical school, and it seemed natural that our conversation would focus on the science and the medical facts. They seemed real. Safe.

I wanted to drop the role of medical student and talk about what it meant, rather than how it worked. Part of me was afraid to talk about how it felt, but the rest of me wanted to. I got the sense that she'd welcome an emotional connection. But instead, we both stared at the picture of my daughter's chromosomes. I couldn't tell if we were hiding behind our professional identities or using them as supports.

Her eyes held a thin film of tears. Or maybe I was just imagining the tears.

I tiptoed back into Sally's hospital room. She was still resting, her eyes closed. Sarah was asleep inside the molded, curving swoops of plexiglass, atop a stainless steel stand, the entire setup designed for ease in disinfecting. The light diffused into her cradle, and the shadows were soft. I stood over her, and for a moment saw perfection in the whorls of her ears, small and discreet, close to her scalp. And then Sarah's slanted eyelids fluttered in her sleep, and I no longer saw perfection.

The vinyl chair made a soft whooshing sound when I sat. Sally opened her eyes.

"They're smaller than I expected," I said.

"Smaller?"

"The 21st chromosomes." It felt silly, saying that a microscopic structure was smaller than I had expected. But I was feeling something else, too: it involved not liking myself very much and wishing that, after running my fingers across the cutouts of my daughter's chromosomes, I'd come back and touched her fingers, or forearm. Stroked her cheek. Bent down to smell her fine and downlike hair. A better father would have lingered just a few more moments beside her cradle.

But this infant did not seem like my child. Staring into

Sarah's face, I wanted to see something of my wife or me: Sally's eyes or her strong jawline, or my nose—any little trait that would link her to our families. I wanted to love her, accept her. But I felt more connection to my daughter's chromosomes than I did to her sleeping face.

Chapter Five

The afternoon sun angled through the window of our apartment's living room in married student housing. Sally sat on a rattan couch, with Sarah at her breast. Sarah was making contented sounds. The cinderblock walls, painted a glossy white, reflected the midwinter light. The yellow cushions of the couch seemed to glow in the incandescent light from the lamp next to Sally. A framed poster by Van Gogh hung on the wall—a row of farmhouses, blue and white, with thatched roofs, lined up against a yellow sky.

Our apartment consisted of a kitchenette with a Formica counter and glossy white plywood cabinets, two small bedrooms, and a tiny bath. Steel door frames and casement windows. The floors—brown linoleum tiles over concrete—felt chilly to bare feet, summer and winter. The corners of the tiles curled slightly in the area under the living room window.

On the kitchen windowsill, Sally had perched three small terracotta pots: a bulbous emerald rubber plant, another plant with green and red variegations, and one with leaves like tiny elephant ears. In the sink was a plastic bathing tub, ergonomically shaped to hold a baby in a seated, reclining position. Sarah looked like a fleshy little astronaut, splashing and laughing. The kitchen smelled of baby shampoo. After her bath, Sally wrapped her in a white terrycloth drying blanket with a triangular pocket sewn into the corner, embroidered with a mouse's eyes and nose, and with small yellow ears with blue piping at the edges. The pocket functioned as a hat, and Sarah was damp on Sally's shoulder, the top of her head covered with the mouse's face, the ears sticking up. Sarah's eyes were bright—such delight in a bath, in a terrycloth blanket.

Sarah's room had a crib and a wooden tool chest I had made when I was a carpenter in my midtwenties. It was four and a half feet long, and two feet wide. With a two-inch foam pad that Sally had covered with blue Naugahyde; it was the perfect height for a changing table. I cleaned Sarah, put her in fresh, dry diapers. With her tummy full and her diapers dry, she seemed content. I laid her in her crib, and touched the mobile clamped to the side rail. She watched the tiny pastel elephants making slow and bobbing circles above her head.

Back in our room, the sheets were crumpled and warm,

and there was a fine scrim of frost on the windows. Sally tucked an absorbent disk of cotton in her bra, nestling it against her nipple. After five months of breastfeeding, Sally's movements were deft and routine. Her bras had always been colorful, wispy things: her breasts compact, not requiring the industrial truss work of heavier cup sizes. Now she wore stiff, white, functional bras, with wide straps and multiple hooks, designed for heft and support.

"I can take her for a walk," I said. "Let you sleep in."

"Thanks." Sally yawned and stretched her arms. "That would be great." She scrunched down into bed and pulled the comforter over her shoulders. "Everything should be in the diaper bag." As a fourth-year medical student, I was doing rotations in the hospital, and it was a rare and happy occasion to have a weekend in which I wasn't on call either day.

When we were inside the apartment, I noticed the delight on Sarah's face more than the slant of her eyes. She and Sally and I were our own little family. We laughed with Sarah as she splashed the water in the tub, or after she had fed and let loose a raspy belch. At five months old, Sarah could hold her head up when she was lying on her belly, and could sit propped up against the yellow cushions on the couch in her blue and white striped OshKosh engineer's bibs. She laughed easily, and was always glad to see me or Sally.

But when I stepped outside our home with Sarah, I felt

that I needed to arrange my face: keep my lips pulled up
in an unchanging smile, in preparation for well-meaning
comments and innocent questions that people might have.
More often than not, people didn't even notice us, but I still
felt as if I were on stage—chosen by God, or the cosmos, or
random chance, to have a child who was so different.

Yet on that day, I felt ready, even eager, to leave our
warm, safe home and take my daughter on a walk in the
brisk air. I bundled Sarah in a puffy zippered snowsuit and
a cap that Sally's mom had knitted. The stroller was a burgundy canvas hand-me-down from one of Sally's friends. It
was a bulky thing, with gray plastic wheels that wobbled at
a certain speed.

In the cold air, Sarah's cheeks turned pink. The sun was
bright, and the bare limbs of oak trees were a stark black
against a brilliant sky. A few papery brown leaves still cling-
ing to the branches fluttered and rattled in the breeze. I
tucked the blanket around Sarah. We walked past the connected buildings of the hospital, a rambling maze of addi-
tions and add-ons, toward the campus of the University of
North Carolina. Past the football stadium and the belltower
parking lot.

The wheels of the stroller jittered along the brick walkways. I was glad it was early on a Saturday, so I wouldn't have
to thread my way past throngs of undergraduates moving

with confidence and purpose. At the heart of the campus, I walked past the Graduate Library: built of gray limestone, it had a domed roof and a wide flight of stairs leading up to fluted columns. Inside was my favorite place to study: wide oak tables, marble columns, oak card catalogues with long skinny drawers and small brass knobs.

I was glad the quad was empty, and there were no students throwing footballs or Frisbees. I had never mastered the casual snap of the wrist that would launch such a smooth and weightless glide, or the loose-limbed wait for the arrival. I was always too self-conscious to learn to play that way.

Sarah and I walked past the building where I'd taken physics, and past the art department. We cut down an alley to Franklin Street. I peeked in on Sarah. She was sleeping. We crossed Franklin, walked to Rosemary, turned left, and walked a few more blocks.

I had always liked Breadmen's Restaurant: plywood booths, sunflower-seed bread, and breakfast all day long. The waitresses wore jeans and T-shirts. I shrugged off my jacket and slid into a booth. Paige, our server, had long auburn hair pulled back into a clasp. A wisp of hair had escaped, and curled down the side of her neck. She poured coffee, took my order, and bent over to peek into the stroller. "What's her name?" Her voice was a whisper.

"Sarah," I whispered back. "We're letting her mother sleep in."

"Good man." She gave me a thumbs-up, and looked back into the stroller. She opened her eyes wider. "Are we awake?"

I leaned over and looked into the buggy. Sarah gazed up at me, and then at Paige.

"Such beautiful eyes." Paige's voice was soft. Sincere. She lingered a moment to look at Sarah, and then straightened back up and poured another dollop of coffee into my mug. "Food'll be out in a minute," she said.

Sarah and I stared at each other. I wondered if Paige had a sister or brother with Down syndrome. Or maybe she just thought that Sarah's eyes were pretty. Sarah stared at her fingers and then put them in her mouth.

I went to the rack at the front of the restaurant and got a paper. Back in the booth, I opened it to the editorial page, enjoying the smell of the newsprint and ink, the chilly surface of the newspaper. Other people came in, and through the open door brought a shiver of cold air with them, making the humid warmth of the restaurant feel even more delicious. I looked at Sarah and wondered if she was too warm. I zipped open her jacket. She watched me.

I ate, read the paper, and sipped my coffee. Sarah dozed again. I left a big tip for Paige, bundled Sarah again, and pushed the stroller outside. *Such beautiful eyes*. A stranger had seen beauty in my daughter's face. I felt a swelling in my chest, as if something was expanding there.

I sat on a bus stop bench and took slow, deep breaths.

Sarah's eyes were closed. Open or closed, they always slanted. Always looked like Down syndrome. Mentally retarded.*

I didn't know how to feel the loss of something that had never happened. I never got to meet the normal infant we'd been waiting for. Neither did Sally. It was as if we were standing on an empty railway platform watching a train rumble away, and it was taking our baby with it. A different child had been left behind for us to take care of.

---

* The word "retarded" has become a derogatory term and is rejected by people in the intellectual disability community. When Sarah was born, the term was still used as a medical term. The use of this word, and the word "normal," will be addressed later in the book.

Chapter Six

"How functional will she be?" Priscilla, the intern on the pediatric surgery team, asked. Her question was for Rick, our senior resident. We had just left the room of an infant who was a few days post-op from heart surgery. The girl's name was Madison. She had Down syndrome. I was still a fourth-year medical student—a subintern in this small clump of young doctors in green scrubs and white coats, walking down the hallway of the pediatric ward.

I hadn't told the team that my one-year-old daughter had Down syndrome. Some of my classmates knew. But on the pediatric surgery service, I was the only fourth-year student. I'd kept my mouth shut about my personal life.

Madison was recovering from a VSD repair—an operation which involves cutting the breastbone in half, stopping the heart, slicing it open, and sewing a small patch over a hole in the wall between the bottom two chambers of the heart. Heart defects are more common in children with Down syndrome than those without it. Unlike Madison's,

Sarah's heart defects were small and unlikely to cause her any problems.

We were on work rounds: our attending—a professor of pediatric surgery—wasn't with us. I liked work rounds because they were less formal, and you could ask a question without feeling stupid. You got the real scoop.

"If things go well," Rick, the senior resident said without breaking stride, "the only thing left will be the scar. Maybe a faint murmur that no one can hear." He flipped the three-by-five card to the back of his sack. "Next we have . . ."

"What I mean is," Priscilla stopped walking. "With the Down syndrome. How functional will she be?"

"She'll make a good pet." Rick didn't slow his pace.

———

In the movies, the dad of a child with Down syndrome would never let a comment like "She'll make a good pet" go by uncontested. Movie dads say things like, "In our house, we call it Up syndrome." The Hollywood dads celebrate each small triumph. First smile, first word, and first awkward step. A tear may streak down his cheek as he picks up a small crutch or tucks his child in at night, but a Hollywood dad is never ashamed of a special needs child.

Of course, some movie dads are louts. During the opening credits a father may abandon the damaged child, so the audience can settle into a story about a single mom who faces the challenges of a special-needs child alone. We like to think we'd be like her: loving and strong. We know we'd never look as good as a Hollywood mom, her morning hair never messy, as she stands in her robe, clutching her child to her chest. But we would hold our baby and claim her with the same fierce love.

Rick stopped at room 534. One of my patients. He looked at each of us, his eyebrows raised. Rick was always clean-shaven and had meticulously brushed hair, no matter the time of day or night. He had a Mont Blanc pen and a stainless steel diver's watch with dials and bezels and a heavy steel band. He used a Littmann Cardiology III stethoscope—three hundred dollars. Most of the residents used the fifty-dollar scope they'd bought in medical school.

"This one's mine," I said. The prevailing wisdom among the residents was, *Give me a medical student who doesn't triple my work, and I'll kiss his ass.* I had no illusion about how little I knew about the practical things of medicine. I just hoped not to embarrass myself. "Post-op day three," I started off. "Status-post resection of intussusception, end-to-end anastamosis. Doing well." If Rick wanted more information, I was ready. I had most of the lab values committed to memory, and all of them were on my three-by-five card. I could feel my heart beating faster.

He made a rolling motion with his hand to tell me to keep going.

"Labs look good, incision is clean. We're waiting for flatulence, and will start clear liquids as soon as we hear it." Priscilla, my intern, had prepped me well. As her medical student, I fetched her things: tracked down x-rays and lab reports. She liked Diet Coke. I brought her one if I went to the cafeteria on a coffee run. She, in turn, taught me how the ward worked: how to give just the right amount of information to an attending, a senior resident.

Rick nodded, satisfied. He slipped the card to the back of his stack and started walking. We followed. Rick was blunt, but he wasn't a bad guy. He wouldn't have made the comment about the child with Down syndrome being a good pet if he'd known about my daughter.

———

A month previously, when I was rotating through internal medicine, I took care of an eighty-nine-year-old woman from a nursing home. She had stopped eating and drinking.

Her closest relative, who lived in another state, insisted that the doctors do everything possible to keep her alive. A general surgeon made a hole in her abdominal wall and poked a thin rubber feeding tube into her stomach, and stitched it in place.

Contractures pulled the woman's arms and legs into an inflexible fetal pose. Pale skin was stretched tight against her elbows and knees. Bedsores from the nursing home eroded the flesh at her hips, all the way to the bone—big red craters with a thin, bubbly yellow drainage that smelled of rotten meat. Her eyes were open, but they never moved or blinked beneath the delicate curve of the bony orbits of the eyes.

In spite of the feeding tube, she continued to lose weight. The contours of her skull were starkly visible; the zygomatic arches were prominent over her sunken cheeks. Her papery, hooded eyelids were wrinkled like a lizard's, and her corneas were a milky white. Her tongue and lips were dry and cracked. She had one lone tusk of a yellow canine tooth. The bones of her back lined up precisely, like the tines of an abandoned farm machine. Thin, dark stool leaked from the edges of her blue plastic diaper.

I tried to imagine what she had been like twenty years ago, when she could still talk and laugh, and track with her eyes the movement in the room. But when I knew her, the only movement was her breathing—as regular as a slow-moving piston, a wheezing sound, accompanied by the rattle of a stubborn chunk of phlegm. Her skinny shoulders hunched in rhythm with her breathing.

She didn't seem human.

But who was I to say that someone was not human? Isn't that what Hitler said about the Jews and what segregationists said about African Americans: *They are a different species. Sub-human.* But standing in that room, permeated by the scent of talcum powder and liquid stool, the woman's desiccated body seemed little more than the husk of a person.

I did what I could. I gave her intravenous fluids and monitored her electrolytes: sodium and potassium. I carefully tracked the blood urea nitrogen and creatinine. Her care became an exercise in fluid and electrolyte balance. Too little fluid, and she might go further into kidney failure. Too much fluid, and it would overload her heart, and the fluid would back up into her lungs.

Twice a day I listened to the steady thump of her heart and the rattling excursions of her lungs. When I touched her, I did so gently. I spoke to her in a soft voice, hoping that she would understand the tone, if not the words. Then I'd hustle on to the next patient, glad to be free of her rasping presence. Otherwise, I avoided seeing her.

John Locke, in his *Essay Concerning Human Understanding*, published in 1690, wrestled with the question of what makes us human. In doing so, he laid the groundwork for modern psychology.

I admired Locke and was inclined to agree with most of what he wrote. He was a physician, studied respiration and circulation, and he knew men like Robert Boyle, Thomas Willis, and Robert Hooke: giants in science and medicine. Locke's philosophical writing started the Enlightenment and his political writing shaped the American Constitution. Voltaire was a fan: "Perhaps no man ever had a more judicious or more methodical genius, or was a more acute logician than Mr. Locke."[13]

In the *Essay Concerning Human Understanding*, Locke discussed the differences between humans and other animals—horses, donkeys, monkeys, parrots, and oysters— and concluded that the ability to understand abstract ideas makes a human's soul different from a beast's. A dog, for instance, may recognize his owner, but would not be able to understand the abstract notion of ownership.

"Beasts abstract not," he wrote.

As Locke teased out the subtleties of the argument, he used the insane and imbecilic as test cases. He considered the minds of imbeciles as being too sluggish and clumsy to generate abstract thoughts. The insane, he thought, had active, nimble minds, and were able to join two simple thoughts to form a more complex and abstract one, but they did so imperfectly. He implied that the insane seemed closer to being fully human than the imbecilic.[14] "What will your driveling, unintelligent intractable Changeling be? Shall a defect in the Body make a Monster; a defect in the Mind, (the far more Noble, and in the common phrase, the far more Essential Part) not?"[15]

It's not surprising that a man with a knack for abstract thought might choose reason as the dividing line between human and less than human. A poet may just as easily assert that expressing oneself in metered verse is the truest test for someone's humanity. A musician may consider perfect pitch the sine qua non, and an NBA star may feel that hitting a half-court shot at the buzzer is the pinnacle of human achievement: humanity's truest test.

The suspicion that Locke would consider my daughter less than human was like a splinter in the sole of my foot as I winced through the rest of his essay, head down, feeling defensive for my child who'd be fenced in with the horses, parrots, and oysters of John Locke's schema.

I tossed the book aside. Fuck John Locke. And fuck his "Beasts abstract not." Sarah might never be an abstract thinker. She might track more toward the physical and practical. The earthbound. She might not be able to compute the degree of consanguinity between aunts and uncles, nieces and nephews, but on a family beach vacation, at the age of twenty-two, she would bring along a suitcase of clothes and DVDs for herself and a duffel bag filled with plastic buckets and shovels and toys for her younger cousins.

In Tolstoy's *The Death of Ivan Ilyich*, the dying magistrate found no enlightenment through words or abstract thoughts: simple acts of kindness from a peasant, and a wordless kiss from his son, pulled Ivan into his full humanity. His redemption came through human touch.

My infant daughter showed her humanity in the way she reflexively grasped my finger in her palm. Later, she would show it in the way she slumped up against me sitting on the couch, or wrinkled her nose when she heard a bad pun. Sarah frowned as she read the label of a container of food, looking for wheat or gluten, to which she was allergic. I didn't need John Locke to tell me if my daughter was human.

But a near-moribund nursing home patient with a thready pulse and rasping respirations, lying in an oversaturated adult diaper? Is she fully human? Or the brain-dead patient in the neurosurgery ICU, a machine pumping air through a tube in his windpipe, his nourishment coming from a tube jabbed down into his stomach, and his urine draining out from a tube snaking up through his penis and into his bladder?

In his book *Less Than Human: Why We Demean, Enslave, and Exterminate Others*, David Livingstone Smith examined the phenomenon of dehumanization.[16] Early in the work, Smith quoted the cultural anthropologist Franz Boas: "Among many primitive people, the only individuals dignified by the term human beings are members of the tribe. It even happens in some cases that language will designate only tribal members as 'he' or 'she,' while all foreigners are 'it.' They are objects or animals."

Smith mentioned that many Native American tribes referred to themselves as "the human beings": Apache, Cheyenne, Chipewyan, Comanche, Yurok, Innu, Klamath, Gwich'in, Mandan, Navajo, Ute. Woven into the language itself was the assumption that all other tribes, all other people, are something other than human. Contemporary German language has a similar construct: *Deutsch* is derived from an Indo-European word meaning "human beings." Smith came to the conclusion that the impulse to dehumanize others is "grounded in biology, culture, and the architecture of the human mind."

If we are quick to see people from other tribes as subhuman, what about people with physical deformities? When we see a typical newborn—with ten precise little fingers and toes, such well-formed lips and eyes—we marvel. A coworker brings an infant to work, and we gather around to admire the child. We whisper in her presence, transfixed by the flawless tiny eyelashes, the perfect little nose.

But a child with a deformity? We try not to gasp, or stare. In Mesopotamia, the fertile land between the Tigris and the Euphrates, humans made the first written record of a birth defect. Scribes recorded what the priests dictated: congenital defects were just one of many types of omens available for analysis. Divination. Prophecy. The flight of a bird, the shape of smoke rising in the air, the liver of a slaughtered lamb, the movement of the stars and moon—each event carried information from the gods.

The births of anomalous children were recorded in cuneiform letters pressed into tablets of clay. Following each description was the interpretation, the prophecy.[17]

> When a woman gives birth to an infant that has the ears of a lion, there will be a powerful king in the country.

> When a woman gives birth to an infant whose nostrils are absent, the country will be in affliction, and the house of the man will be ruined.

> If a woman gives birth to twins joined back to back, the gods will abandon the country, the king and his son will abandon the city.

King Ashurbanipal's royal library in Nineveh, in the eighth century BC, included four tablets of omens relating to sixty-two human congenital malformations, and what each malformation portended. There is no record of the Babylonians killing handicapped children.[18]

This notion—that a congenital defect is a portent, or a warning from the gods—appeared in later cultures as well. The root of the word "monster" is the Latin word *monstrum* (portent, warning, aberrant occurrence) from *monere* (advise, warn). "Monster" meant birth defect. Unlike the Babylonians, the Greeks and Romans sacrificed their monstrous newborns in the hope of appeasing the gods.

In the Middle Ages, children with defects were thought to be the result of sex with animals, or demons, or Satan himself. Martin Luther (1483–1546), when asked about a twelve-year-old with bizarre behavior, suggested that she was a changeling (the child of a demon that had been swapped for a normal child) and could therefore be drowned, because she did not have a soul.[19]

Michel de Montaigne (1533–92) had a different take on "monstrous" children. Montaigne is considered by many to be the father of the modern essay, and his *Essais*—French for "attempts" or "trials"—followed wherever his thoughts took him.[20] In the two-page piece "Of a Monstrous Child," he related his experience of seeing a pair of twins conjoined at the chest: one head, two lower bodies. "In all other respects," Montaigne wrote, "he was of ordinary shape; he could stand on his feet, walk, and prattle about like others of the same age. He had not been willing to take any other nourishment than from his nurse's breast; and what they tried to put in his mouth in my presence he chewed on a little and spat it out without swallowing. There seemed indeed to be something peculiar about his cries. He was just fourteen months old. Below the breast he was fastened and stuck to another child, without a head, and with his spinal canal stopped up, the rest of his body being entire. For indeed one arm was shorter, but it had been broken accidentally at their birth. They were joined face to face, and as if a smaller child were trying to embrace a bigger one around the neck . . . thus the connection was between the nipples and the navel. The navel of the imperfect child could not be seen, but the rest of his belly could. In this way all of this imperfect child that was not attached, as the arms, buttocks, thighs, and legs, remained hanging and dangling on the other and might reach halfway down his legs. The nurse also told us that he urinated from both places."

Montaigne described the child for a few more lines, and then wrote:

This double body and these several limbs, connected with a single head, might well furnish a favorable prognostic to the king that he will maintain under the union of his laws these various parts and factions of our state. But for fear the event should belie it, it is better to let it go its way, for there is nothing like divining about things past.

So that, when things have happened, by some interpretation they are found to have been prophesied. [Cicero]. As they said of Epimenides that he prophesied backwards.

"I have just seen a shepherd in Medoc," Montaigne continued, "thirty years old or thereabouts, who has no sign of genital parts. He has three holes by which he continually makes water. He is bearded, has desire, and likes to touch women." Montaigne goes on:

What we call monsters are not so to God, who sees in the immensity of his work the infinity of forms that he has comprised in it; and it is for us to believe that this figure that astonishes us is related and linked to some other figure of the same kind unknown to man. From his infinite wisdom there proceeds nothing but that is good and ordinary and regular; but we do not see its arrangement and relationship. What he sees often, he does not wonder at, even if he does not know why it is. *If something happens which he has not seen before, he thinks it is a prodigy* [Cicero]. . . .

We call contrary to nature what happens contrary to custom; nothing is anything but according to nature, whatever it may be. Let this universal and natural reason drive out of us the error and astonishment that novelty brings us.[21]

Where Locke created an abstract line between humans and beasts, Montaigne challenged us to question our assumptions about what we observe around us. He suggested that all of us are "good and ordinary and regular," if perceived correctly.

In 1641, a one-eyed pig was born in New Haven, Connecticut. A local swineherd had the misfortune of having "one eye for use, the other hath (as itt is called) a pearle in itt," and the townspeople thought that the young man's opaque eye resembled the eye of the malformed piglet, and came to the conclusion that the cycloptic pig was the result of an "unnatureall spell and abominable filthyness" of the swineherd. The young man's trial lasted from 1641 to 1642. He was executed on April 8, 1642. They killed the pig by running a sword through it, in front of the young man, just prior to his execution.[22]

Club feet, shortening of the upper extremities, long and deformed ears, syndactylism (fused toes or fingers), were all thought to be proof of Satanic origin.[23] In Copenhagen in 1683, a girl who gave birth to a monster with "a cat's head" was burned alive.[24]

Even in modern times, some people see a message from God in the physical traits of newborns. In February 2010, Virginia state delegate Robert Marshall said that God punishes parents who have had abortions by making subsequent children disabled. After an outpouring of anger from parents of children with disabilities, he apologized and said that his remarks had been misconstrued.[25] As a politician, he pretty much had to; most people these days see a birth defect as a medical condition, not a message from God. Of course, after reading Montaigne, one might question the very notion of "birth defect": "We call contrary to nature what happens contrary to custom; nothing is anything but according to nature, whatever it may be. Let this universal and natural reason drive out of us the error and astonishment that novelty brings us."

But what about severe defects? Sally told me of a malformed child she saw when she was working on the labor and delivery ward: the intern delivered the baby and then the placenta, and left the room without speaking. The intern couldn't help it: she had begun to vomit behind her surgical mask. "The baby was an anencephalic." Sally placed her hand even with her eyebrows. "Nothing above here, except a mass of pulpy red tissue. The intern's hands mushed right into it."

There's a website with information on anencephaly, written by parents of children with the condition.[26] They tell the stories of pregnancy and birth. There are photographs of mothers in patterned hospital johnnies and fathers in green OR scrubs cradling their stillborn or soon-to-die infant.

The infants all wear the small knit caps that newborns wear, covering the absence of the top half of the head. In most of the snapshots the mother and father manage to smile.

Science has freed most of us from medieval superstition: we no longer burn a woman at the stake for giving birth to a child with anomalies, and parents can hold a child with anencephaly without the risk of execution for "abominable filthyness." For this we can thank scientists like Tjio, who gave us the first clear photograph of a human karyotype, and doctors like Gautier and Lejeune, who discovered the link between Down syndrome and trisomy 21.

But the division Locke proposed between "humans" and "beasts [who] abstract not" continues to echo in the modern geneticist's division between "normal child" and "abnormal fetus," as if there is a binary system, like a light switch that is either on or off. But human qualities exist on a spectrum. Whether we measure IQ points, the amount of melanin in the skin, or some degree of "ability," human characteristics are rarely all or none. What is it that compels us to draw a line beyond which we consider someone else abnormal?

During the rest of work rounds Rick listened intently to every detail of each patient's status, and made suggestions on what we should do next—advance the child's diet from clear liquids to a mechanical-soft diet, or check a child's electrolytes. As we walked from room to room, he joked with the team and talked about basketball.

When we finished work rounds, we split up to write orders, check on x-rays, and follow up on lab results. I thought about going back to Madison's room, maybe show her mom a picture of my daughter, Sarah—the one in which she is putting on an extra-large Santa hat, the red velvet and white fur trim dwarfing her face. And I could tell her about another mom I knew, with a daughter named Clarissa; we'd met her at a Down syndrome support group.

Clarissa had had a VSD like Madison's. One surgeon, a caring man who listened well, had told Clarissa's mom that she was too young for the surgery, that she should wait several months. At a different hospital, and after a very brief assessment, another surgeon told her that it was dangerous to wait; Clarissa would get weaker the longer they delayed. This second surgeon was young and cocky and wore French cuffs with gold cufflinks under his white coat, and a gold Rolex. Clarissa's parents lived in the country, and grew their own organic vegetables. They mistrusted Western medicine. Clarissa's mother didn't like the young guy's Brooks Brothers wardrobe or his manner of speaking, which seemed off-hand, almost flippant. But his confidence was compelling. They scheduled the surgery.

Clarissa's mom talked about her post-op course in terms of miracles: Clarissa began to breastfeed more vigorously, and gained weight quickly. She had better muscle tone. "And within a few weeks, her hair started growing. All this came out so suddenly," she said, fluffing Clarissa's hair. "I hadn't expected that."

I walked past Madison's room without stopping. My thoughts were too confused and my feelings too close to the surface to risk talking with the girl's parents.

———

When the surgical team was on teaching rounds—when an attending was with us—we all trooped into the room and the resident presented the patient: a few salient points about the history, the surgical procedure, and the status of the child. Most of the patients on this ward had a problem with a single organ: a heart defect to patch, a tight place in the digestive tract that required excision. With successful surgery, they would lead normal lives.

We spoke in lowered voices. Sometimes the mother's eyes would glance from her infant lying in the hospital bed to each of us. When it happened, I never knew what she was looking for. Reassurance? Connection? Perhaps she was hoping for some sign that her child was more than just an illness, an anatomical abnormality.

We stood mute, and listened. The attending would usually touch the child: either listen to the chest with a stethoscope, or peel back a bandage to look at the wound. Then he would nod, and we'd all walk out. He'd always pause at the door and speak with the mother. Out in the hallway, he'd ask us questions, to find out what we knew and didn't know, about this particular case or the disease process in general. He'd then ask the senior resident to explain it to us. Although being put on the spot in front of our friends and peers was miserable, it wasn't nearly as bad as meeting the gaze of a worried mother.

———

The next morning, on attending rounds, we filed into Madison's room. She looked like a small, frail version of my daughter—the same gentle slant to her eyes, the same small nose.

Rick gave a brief summary of the girl's post-op course. Dr. Rankin, the attending, bent over and listened to the heart. The girl's mother watched.

"Sounds good," he said, folding his stethoscope and slipping it into the pocket of his long white coat.

The girl's mother smiled and then glanced at each of us. Her eyes met mine. I wished there were a secret handshake, or a coded message I could give her. *My daughter has Down syndrome too.* But I was still uncertain of my role—I wasn't a doctor yet and I didn't know how much self-disclosure was acceptable. Sometimes the boundaries serve the doctor; sometimes they serve the patient. In this case, I didn't know which was which.

Chapter Seven

"My cousin is Downs." A woman I'd never seen before was bending over my shopping cart peering down at Sarah, who was asleep in a baby carrier.

I was standing in the checkout line of the grocery store, looking at the cover of a *Cosmopolitan* magazine, curious to know more about "Long Term Lusty Sex: Taking the Monotony Out of Monogamy." Sally and I had been married for six years. We'd never bored each other in bed, but still . . .

I glanced a couple of times at the conveyor belt—the stacks of frozen pizzas, tubes of refrigerator biscuits, and six-packs of Diet Coke ahead of my purchases. The woman leaning over my shopping cart was about my age, maybe a few years older, and several pounds heavier. "And he is an angel," the woman continued, still looking down at Sarah. "A perfect angel." The roots of her blond hair were dark. Her scalp was pink. She straightened. The top few buttons of her blouse were undone.

I bobbed my head and smiled in acknowledgment. It would have been presumptuous to correct her. But it wasn't just poor grammar to say he *is* Down syndrome. He must be something more than a diagnosis. And anyway, it was Saturday afternoon, and I was just a guy in a pair of jeans and a T-shirt getting a six-pack of St. Pauli Girl beer and some Triscuits. I wanted to let someone else represent the Down syndrome community.

"You and your wife must be pretty special," the woman said. "For God to choose you two to raise this little angel." She looked me in the eye. Her eyelids were a shimmering blue.

In 1953 Dale Evans wrote a book called *Angel Unaware* about her daughter, Robin, who had Down syndrome.[27] Against the advice of the doctors, Dale and her husband, Roy Rogers, decided to "keep" her, and take her home. At the time, doctors routinely recommended that mongoloids be put away. "You don't want to get too attached," the doctors told Dale and Roy. "It will only break your heart. This baby will never have a normal life, she will never live past two years of age, she will never be able to read or do anything else. Besides," the doctors continued, "the baby won't know the difference anyway. She won't even remember you from one visit to another."[28]

Dale Evans and Roy Rogers were international celebrities with public personas that were as carefully crafted as the characters they played in the movies. In 1943, Roy was featured on the cover of *Life* magazine. The full-page photograph showed him relaxed in the saddle as his horse reared up on a mountaintop. The article described the character that Roy played: "He is purity rampant—never drinks, never smokes, never shoots pool, never spits, and the roughest oath at his command is 'shucks!'" The report continued, "Roy actually doesn't smoke and he never takes a drink in public."[29] Roy's image was on everything from binoculars to boots. In one year alone, 900,000 Roy Rogers lunchboxes, 1,203,000 jeans and jackets, and two million comic books and records were sold.

In her memoir, *Cowboy Princess: Life with My Parents Roy Rogers and Dale Evans*, Cheryl Rogers-Barnett writes, "I didn't realize at the time how courageous they were in taking this stand—the studio was very upset with them. To the public relations department, a child with Down syndrome was the ultimate in bad publicity. They were convinced that Mom and Dad would repel their fans by 'flaunting' this sick child. Even the people at church disapproved. Some of them believed—and even said aloud—that a child with a handicap was a punishment, that the parent had clearly committed some terrible sin and this child was the result."

The studio had a point about the brand's public image: this was a time in which "ugly laws," written to keep unsightly people from going out in public, were still in existence. The most famous example was part of the Chicago municipal code, passed in 1911 and repealed in 1974: "No person who is diseased, maimed, mutilated or in any way deformed so as to be an unsightly or disgusting object or improper person to be allowed in or on the public ways or other public places in this city, shall therein or thereon expose himself to public view, under a penalty of not less than one dollar nor more than fifty dollars for each offense."[30] Chicago was far from an isolated example: San Francisco, Portland, Denver, Omaha, and Reno all had "ugly laws" on the books. The state of Pennsylvania passed a state version of the law.

The *smart* thing for Roy and Dale to do would have been to hide the child away.

Pearl S. Buck, the Pulitzer-Prize winning author of *The Good Earth* and Nobel laureate, spent thirty years denying the existence of Carol, her daughter with intellectual disabilities.[31]

At first, Carol had seemed like any other child, but she began to express her wants "with jabbering and grunts, sniffing at visitors or jumping up at them like a dog."[32] Buck writes, "She was three years old when I first began to wonder." She took Carol to physician after physician, hoping to find the cause of the child's failure to develop. Eventually she took her to the Mayo Clinic, where one of the doctors said, "You will wear out your life and beggar your family unless you give up hope and face the truth. This child will be a burden to you all your life. Get ready to bear that burden."

Buck would later write, "I can remember those words exactly as he spoke them. I suppose the shock photographed them upon my memory. I remember too, exactly how he looked, a little man, shorter than I, his face pale, a small, clipped black mustache, under which his lips were grim. He looked cruel, but I know he was not. I know now that he suffered while he spoke."[33] She referred to the exchange as a "moment for which I shall be grateful as long as I live." She decided to put the child away.

After visiting multiple state and private institutions, Buck found one with a director she trusted, the Vineland Training School. Dr. Edward Johnstone's philosophy was: "The only child who can learn is a happy child." Even so, it was a difficult decision to leave Carol there. "Only the thought of a future with a child grown old and me gone kept me from hurrying to the railway station."

Carol was born in 1920, during the height of the eugenics

movement. Part pseudoscience and part social reform movement, eugenics aimed to breed better humans. A child with
mental retardation was seen as indelible proof of hidden
faults in the bloodline: alcoholism, drug addiction, sloth,
or sluttiness. A disabled child brought shame to the family.

Mainstream magazines like *Collier's* ran articles about
eugenics. This was a magazine for sophisticated, educated
readers: Winston Churchill, Ernest Hemingway, F. Scott
Fitzgerald, J. D. Salinger, and John Steinbeck all wrote for
the magazine. The advertisements were for upscale whiskey,
GE refrigerators, and Nash automobiles.

Past issues of *Collier's* are collectable now for the vibrant
original artwork on the covers. The issue of May 20, 1939,
has an illustration that is clever and stylish and fills the
entire cover. Across the bottom, in bold block print, it
reads: "LEGALIZE MERCY KILLINGS! By Dr. Foster Kennedy." Dr. Kennedy, a well-known neurologist and
eugenicist, believed in euthanizing "defective" children. He
wrote, "I am opposed to the legalization of euthanasia for
those persons who, having been well, are now ill. I believe it
would be for the general good that euthanasia be legalized
for creatures born defective, whose present condition is miserable and whose future, in the opinion of a properly con-
stituted board acting under state authority, is hopeless."[34]

A couple of years later, Dr. Kennedy wrote an editorial

in the *American Journal of Psychiatry*, specifying that the defective children should not be killed before five years of age, because in some cases, it took that long to determine if the defects were severe and permanent.[35]

Germany was the only modern country that went so far as to kill defective children, but eugenicists in the United States made disabled children a source of personal shame. When the Nazi war crimes were exposed at the Nuremberg trials, eugenics lost much of its popular support in the United States. But the notion that a child with intellectual disabilities exposed a secretly tainted bloodline was slow to fade. It's easy to see how Buck would deny her daughter.

But in May of 1950, she went public about Carol in a feature article titled "The Child Who Never Grew," for *Ladies' Home Journal*. She later expanded it into a book of the same title.[36] In the book, she was honest about her ambivalence about her daughter. While she considered the idea of killing disabled children "monstrous," she admitted that "it is inevitable that one ponders much on the matter of a kindly death."

———

Not Dale Evans. She cherished Robin until she died from encephalitis just before turning two years old.[37] Dale began *Angel Unaware* a few days later. This short book is written as if it was a letter from Robin to God, reviewing the mission God had assigned to Robin: to enrich the spiritual lives of her parents. The book came out in 1953, five years before Lejeune would discover the extra copy of the chromosome that causes Down syndrome.

I could accept the idea that a God may exist—the one I'd learned about in Sunday school. A God who has counted every hair on my head, and who knows when every sparrow falls. I could accept a God who'd know how many dimples there are on a golf ball, and how may grains of sand are in the desert. I could see how that type of deity could be believable. But I couldn't imagine an omniscient deity choosing, on purpose, to "send down a child with Down syndrome." And I couldn't imagine how He would do it: would He send the extra 21st chromosome down like a tiny bolt of lightning? Would the woman's belly twitch from the impact as the special little angel bumped a normal kid out of the way? I just couldn't believe that.

But Dale Evans could, and she wrote a brave book, which sold over 500,000 copies. Evans donated all of the proceeds to the National Association for Retarded Citizens, which allowed them to establish an office. The organization later changed their name to the Association for Retarded Citizens, and was later known as the ARC. When the medical term "retarded" became pejorative, they changed the name to The Arc, dropping the offensive word.

After *Angel Unaware* was published, whenever Dale and

Roy appeared at rodeos or other public appearances, there would always be children with Down syndrome in the audience, clapping and laughing, out in public with their families.

———

"My aunt kept him," the woman said as she handed the checkout guy some cash. "He's thirty-two. Watches TV with her." She turned back to face me. "Can't read a lick, but he loves *Kojak*. He can go through a TV guide and put his finger on every single *Kojak*." Her voice carried a note of pride. She put her change in her pocketbook and snapped it shut. Her high-heeled shoes made sharp clicking sounds as she pushed her cart away.

Chapter Eight

In a genetics journal, I read about a painting that included one of the earliest depictions of a person with Down syndrome.[38] The painting was a Nativity scene—*The Adoration of the Christ Child*—by an unknown painter, and among the angels and shepherds were two with Down syndrome. The shepherd was a "maybe," but both doctors writing the article agreed that for the angel, the diagnosis was clear.

After learning of the painting, I began to read about Early Netherlandish art. I wanted to be confident that the angel with Down syndrome was not a mistake. I studied books from the Duke University library and the Metropolitan Museum of Art, and learned that while Leonardo da Vinci and Michelangelo, in Italy, were creating formal compositions of heroic and ideal beauty, the artists in the Netherlands were capturing, with unprecedented precision, the daily world in which they lived. Brocades and furs, mirrors and glass bottles, were rendered with startling accuracy. The artistic ambition was to capture reality itself, with optical clarity.

During this period, a religious movement that involved using one's imagination to place oneself in the midst of a biblical scene swept through Europe. People would gaze at these breathtakingly realistic paintings—Mary's annunciation, Christ's birth, the Crucifixion—until they were drawn into the scene by innumerable details. The paintings were so real, one could almost feel the warmth coming off of the horses and donkeys, smell the incense and myrrh. In this way, one could have an empathic and emotional experience.[39] Religion became personal.

After reading so much about the nativity painting with the angel with Down syndrome, and staring at a picture of it in a book from the Metropolitan, I felt ready to stand in front of the real thing.

I grabbed an early flight to LaGuardia, took the M–60 bus to Astoria, and the subway from there into Manhattan. Once inside the museum, I clipped the small tin badge to the pocket of my shirt and went to the front desk to ask where I could find the Northern Renaissance paintings. A young woman with long blond hair and tortoiseshell glasses seemed pleased to help, and showed me on a map. I felt a twinge of excitement, and some anxiety.

In the gallery, I recognized other paintings from the book
I'd ordered from the Met—works by Jan van Eyck, Rogier
van der Weyden, and Pieter Bruegel the Elder. I hustled past
annunciations, nativity scenes, and crucifixions, and hurried through the adjacent galleries, glancing at portraits like
faces in a crowd, but the one I wanted to see wasn't there.
I went back to the help desk and flipped through my note
cards for the painting's accession number.

"It's in the Linsky Collection. Gallery 537," the young
woman with the glasses said. "Just past the Watson Library.
Go to the stairs." She made a motion with her hand. "Take
a left and then a right, and go through the piazza, and then
you'll see it."

"Thanks." I slipped through the throngs of visitors and
smiled at the guard at the velvet rope. He glanced at the small
tin badge clipped to my shirt pocket and nodded his head.

I loved the little red badge. This museum.

I walked through the reconstructed patio of a castle built
during the reign of Ferdinand and Isabella, the marble
blocks carefully restacked, the space large and open and
decorated with Italian Renaissance sculptures. I hurried
past a bronze boy plucking a thorn from the sole of his foot,
and past a marble man and woman, naked and struggling.

A guard stood at a doorway, his feet shoulder-width apart
and his hands behind his back.

"Is this the Linsky Collection?" I asked, my voice pitched for a library, or a church.

"What?" He turned his face toward mine. Scowled.

"The Linsky Collection." I glanced at my notes from the help desk. "Gallery 537."

He jerked his thumb toward a number next to the door. "Then I guess this is it." He looked away, shaking his head.

I walked from the brightly lit hall into a darker space—parquet wood floor, pink wallpaper with a maroon heraldic pattern. There were walnut baseboards and wide crown moldings. Off to the side, away from the throngs of visitors, the space felt like a wealthy person's parlor, minus the furniture.

I saw the *Adoration*, and walked to it. Stood. The most striking thing about the painting was the light emanating from the table on which the naked infant lay. Three angels knelt behind the table. Mary knelt at the end, and Joseph stood behind her. He was holding a candle. The angel with Down syndrome was looking over the shoulder of the angel at the center of the painting. She looked young, just like she did in the color photograph in the book. She looked like Sarah.

The faces of the two people closest to the child—Mary and the angel in the center of the painting—were illuminated so brightly that their facial features seemed slightly flattened, the brilliance of the light almost washing out the details. Mary spread her hands above the child as if beholding him with her palms and fingers as well as her eyes. Her hands glowed. The central angel's hands were bright as well, her fingers held together in a steeple.

The light itself was invisible. No rays streamed forth from the baby, no beams, no halos. The light was only present as it reflected against the things and people in the painting: the highlights in Mary's long blond hair, the undersides of the cherubim—baby angels—singing and cavorting overhead, like high stratus clouds illuminated by the morning sun.

This painting, thought to have been done in a shop in Antwerp, Belgium, was a depiction of a vision of Saint Bridget. In her vision she saw a young virgin mother with flowing hair, a naked Christ child, and a chorus of angels singing "sweet and most dulcet songs." She also described a "great and ineffable light" emanating from the Christ child—a "divine splendor [that] totally annihilated the material splendor of the candle" that Joseph held.[40]

I looked over at Joseph, holding the candle in his left hand, shielding it with his right. Sure enough, it was much less bright than the light coming up from baby Jesus. Joseph's sleeves were painted red, his shawl blue-black. Joseph's face, farther from the child than Mary's, was unbleached by the brilliance of the light, and had more nuanced skin tones, with more pinks and browns—the same warm tones as the skin of the angel with Down syndrome, one row back.

The angel with Down syndrome, kneeling between Mary and the central angel, seemed incidental. Unremarkable. Just another witness of something never seen before. I stared at her face—the familiar little upturned nose, the small chin. The eyes.

Five other angels knelt around the baby. The one in the center wore a red brocade tunic and a gold embroidered harness encrusted with gems and rubies. She had blue-feathered wings, held together in repose like a resting butterfly, pointing upward toward the cherubim dancing near the ceiling.

I stared at the painting and let my eyes move freely. They settled on the shepherd who was outside, looking in through a window. In his left hand he held a curved horn. Did he have Down syndrome? His eyes slanted, but were too far apart. I agreed with the article in the genetics journal—it was hard to tell. Behind him, the morning sky showed tiny white stars against a deep and receding blue, and at the horizon a yellow edge of light, the clouds illuminated from below. In the near distance, two shepherds looked up, shielding their eyes from the cool white beams of the star of Bethlehem.

I stepped away from the painting and glanced at the miniature statues in the center of the room. The figures were all

inside plexiglass boxes and lit from above. A bronze satyr
with a thin layer of dark brown lacquer, all hooves and
horns and muscles. Two other satyrs. Hercules with a cud-
gel on one shoulder and a wild boar on the other. A nude
statue of Lucretia, the Roman woman who stabbed herself
in the heart after being raped by the emperor's son.

My eyes were drawn to another Netherlandish painting,
this one from the workshop of Gerard David: *The Adoration of the Magi*. Kneeling men offered gifts to the Christ
child. In the background, two men on horseback crossed
a stream. One horse stopped for a drink. Further back,
a knight rode on horseback, his lance long and thin and
white. A white dog jumped and barked near him. I moved
closer. The brushstrokes were tiny, smaller than the dates on
a penny or a dime. In the distance, blue mountain ranges
receded, their ridges thick with conifers, tiny and sharp. I
leaned closer.

"Step away from the painting." The guard's voice was
harsh, commanding.

I stepped back, and turned my head. "How close can I
get?" I didn't want to break the rules, but there weren't any
velvet ropes, or signs.

"One foot." He pulled his eyebrows together, put his fists
on his hips, and jutted out his chin.

"You sound angry." Years of working in the ER had

taught me to reflect back what I perceived before reacting: I could be seeing something that wasn't there.

"I'm not angry." He scowled. "I just think you already *knew* you were too close."

"No, I didn't. You've educated me." I nodded. "Thanks."

"Huh." He shook his head. Glared at me.

"Look." I turned my body to fully face his. "I'm not looking for a problem, but if you are, we can take this as far as you want." I glanced at his name badge, and back to his face.

"I don't want to take it anywhere," he said. "You were just too close to that painting."

I stared at him for another moment. "Okay." I turned and tried to gauge what twelve inches would be, and looked at the painting some more. My heart was beating hard.

Why was I so quick to anger? What could I have gained by escalating things with a guard in an art museum? I was surprised to find myself so close to the edge where anger jumps past reason. I was standing in a room that swirled with myth and religion: Hercules, Lucretia, and Mary the Mother of God, Nativity scenes conjuring Christmas cards I'd seen all my life. And in this storm of iconography, searching all these faces of gods and babies, women and men, I was looking for confirmation that an artist in the sixteenth century had seen fit to portray someone who looked like my daughter. Never mind that there are forty-five acres of space in the Metropolitan. Two million works of art. And *one* painting that included someone like Sarah.

I took a deep breath, and left the gallery to go to the cafeteria. Maybe after lunch there would be a different guard on duty.

———

That afternoon, I went back to the painting of the angel with Down syndrome, and was struck by the fact that nobody—not Mary, or Joseph, or the angels—was squinting against the too-bright light. The cherubim dancing near the ceiling were laughing and singing, but everyone else had a calm and reverent expression. European noses, narrow and slightly pointed. Thin chins. Lips with subtle upturns, not quite smiling. Except for the angel with Down syndrome. Her nose was wider, stubby. Upturned. Eyes slanting. Lips turned slightly downward. When Sarah's face was relaxed, her lips had the same downward turn, making her look mildly grumpy, or unhappy. "Are you okay?" I'd ask, and she would nod and shrug. "Yeah."

My eyes wandered across the painting, but they always came back to the angel with Down syndrome. I found myself looking at her more intently than the Christ child, or Mother Mary.

This motif—St Bridget's vision of the nighttime adoration of the Christ child—was very popular, and circu-
lated widely. The artist used exquisite verisimilitude; each
and every strand of Mary's hair was rendered, the sheen of
every wave and curl a golden gleam. The cuticle of Mary's
left thumb had a small puffy roll of flesh that we recognize
instantly from seeing our own hands.

I didn't know why the artist had included an angel with
Down syndrome. But it was hard to imagine that it was
an accident. The level of realistic detail was astounding:
the feathers of an angel's wings were crossed and ruffled
from recent flight. The painting had been examined by
infrared reflectography which revealed animated under-
drawing, and pentimenti—changes in the composition,
from the Italian word *pentirsi*, "repent"—indicating that
the artist had changed his mind in the process of painting,
but I couldn't find a reference to pentimenti specific to the
angel's face.[41]

Max Friedländer, a renowned historian of Early Netherlandish art, wrote, "In general, the figures in fifteenth-century
Netherlandish devotional panels are felt to be members of
one family or society, and the donors, introduced by their
patron saints, are admitted as equals into the holy circle."[42]
There's no evidence that this happened with this particular painting, but when one considers the care and precision

with which each detail is rendered, it seems likely that the artist was working from a specific model. A model who happened to have Down syndrome.

I loved this painting, with its richly shadowed interior and the warm bright light shining up from an infant. And I was drawn to this incidental angel, one row back, who looked like my daughter.

Chapter Nine

"You'll turn her into a cripple," I said, staring at the child-sized walker in the center of our living room. For the previous two weeks, Sally had been talking about getting a walker for Sarah, but I'd been against it. Sarah was three years old, and was still not walking. I had finished medical school, and we had moved to Pittsburgh, Pennsylvania, so I could begin residency training in emergency medicine. Sally was taking care of Sarah full time.

Sally took a small step away. She crossed her arms over her chest.

I knew I sounded harsh. But it needed to be said. This small, silent thing wasn't designed for a child like ours: Sarah had Down syndrome, not polio or cerebral palsy. A placid, pretty child, she was always eager to laugh at peek a boo. Sarah slept through the night, and ate whatever we put in front of her.

She was an easy baby and a happy toddler. Only she didn't toddle, or even crawl. Most children crawl at nine months, walk unassisted by the first year. But Sarah, at three years old, sat on the floor, feet together, sole to sole, her muscle tone so loose her knees touched the floor. When she wanted to move, she hitched forward, scooting on her butt. She quickly scuffed through the finish of the leather on the outer surfaces of her shoes—through the gloss of the white dye and into the porous gray of the leather itself. The outer edges of the soles were worn smooth and flat. The bottoms of Sarah's pants were abraded to a gauzy thinness, while the cloth at the knees remained full and thick. It was endearing at first: Sarah's distinctive locomotion.

Sally and I stared at the walker. It was shiny, all curves and cross-braces. I leaned down and picked it up with two fingers of each hand. It was almost weightless. Sarah could lift it without effort. I lowered it back to the floor. Leaned on it. Harder. Tried to twist it. It was solid. Stable. It would not sway or shimmy. It wouldn't tip over.

"Derrick's mother said it helped him learn to walk," Sally said, her arms still tightly crossed under her chest. She uncrossed her arms. "Helped a lot."

"Derrick?"

"He goes to Early Intervention with Sarah," Sally said. "Didn't walk until they got him this." She gestured, palm up, toward the walker.

Sally had enrolled Sarah in Early Intervention when we first moved to Pittsburgh. We were glad that I'd gotten a spot in a residency program there, because the area provided good services for children with Down syndrome. I'd been in medical school at the University of North Carolina when Sarah was born, and there had been plenty of services for children with special needs. We didn't want Sarah to lose the progress she'd made: she could sit unassisted, could grasp a raisin using thumb and forefinger. She could stack blocks. She could feed herself with her fingers.

"The teacher at Early Intervention said it would help, too," Sally said.

I stared at the thing, and tried to listen to what Sally was saying. I was in my second year of residency training, and this month was rotating through internal medicine. It wasn't bad: I only spent every third night in the hospital. The previous night I had been on call, but I'd hustled through my admissions and was able to sneak away to the call room for a nap between 3 and 4 am. Then I'd been paged to the ER to admit a patient in congestive heart failure, but I had managed to treat the patient and do the paperwork and still squeeze in another nap from 5:30 to 6. It hadn't been like the month before, on the trauma service—on call every other night, and going all night when I was there. After such an easy night on call, I should have had some emotional reserve. A more open mind. I should have been able to listen.

"Think of it as a set of training wheels." Sally's voice had a playful lilt. She tilted her head to the side. Sally's eyes crinkled into slits when she smiled, unless she was faking it. This evening there were no crinkles. She angled her head another degree, smiled a bit wider. *Come on. Give it a chance.* At one level, I registered the effort Sally was making to make her voice sound light. To smile. To call a walker "training wheels."

I recognized Sally's effort, and I respected it and I wanted to respond to it. But all I could see was our daughter lurching around the house like a cripple.

We both had tried to teach Sarah to crawl. "See? Like this," I said, on my hands and knees. I moved slowly, isolating each move so she could see. "Can you do it?" Sarah watched. "Can you crawl over here?" I patted the floor in front of me. Sarah smiled as if enjoying the game. She scooted toward me on her butt, her arms raised and parallel to the floor, elbows bent, held forward for balance, as if holding reins. Her movement seemed joyful. Equestrian.

Then we tried to teach her to walk—maybe she could just skip the crawling stage. I made a pull-up bar for Sarah, using cabinet-grade white pine because it has close grain that doesn't splinter. I routed the edges with a quarter-round bit, then sanded everything smooth. The top bar was just above Sarah's waist, a middle bar at the level of her knees. I braced it at the corners, and made a pair of skids that went under a heavy chest in the living room. It was four feet long, rock solid, and worked—sort of. Sarah scooted over to one end of the rack, pulled herself up, and turned to smile at us. Sally and I sat on the floor cross-legged and clapped, "Good job," our voices musical with praise. Sally crawled to the other end of the rail, and held out her hands. "Can you come this way? Just one step?" Sarah's eyes were bright with play and comprehension. She plopped down to her butt, and scooted over to give her mother a hug.

———

"Did signing make her a deaf-mute?" Sally and I were sitting at the tiny square table next to the kitchen window, still arguing about the walker. She leaned forward for her coffee cup. The kitchen walls were a glossy blue, the wood trim had the same dark varnish as the rest of the house. Outside, the evening light was fading.

"No," I admitted. "It didn't." Months previously, I had been against Sarah learning to sign. A speech therapist had told Sally that children learn to speak earlier if they're taught sign language along the way. Not just hearing impaired or intellectually disabled kids—all kids pick up spoken language more quickly if they learn to sign.

"It'll decrease her frustration," Sally had told me. "Just to be able to communicate her needs and wishes." I hadn't been convinced. "Be easier on me, too," Sally said. "If Sarah could just say 'more,'" Sally demonstrated by making bird beaks with the tips of her fingers and thumbs, and gently bumping them against each other, "it would make life so much easier."

But it would make Sarah look deaf, as well as mentally retarded. That was the only objection I could come up with, and even in the moment, I knew I was being stubborn. And stupid.

The speech therapist wore a T-shirt and jeans, with her hair in a long, thick braid almost to her waist. One afternoon she sat cross-legged on the floor, working with Sarah. "The itsy-bitsy spider went up the water spout," the speech therapist said, her hands criss-crossed upward, thumb to forefinger. Sarah watched and moved her hands, too. When the rain came down to wash the spider out, Sarah's fingers fluttered as gently as a spring shower. She sang along, tunelessly and a beat behind, her eyes intent on the speech therapist's fingers.

I watched, and listened.

Sarah quickly learned to sign. After dinner one night, she was sitting in her oak high chair. She had just finished a small bowl of vanilla ice cream. She looked up at Sally, pulled her fingertips to her thumbs, and gently tapped them together. *More.*

Sally shook her head. "No, sweetheart, you've had enough."

Sarah placed her palm flat against her chest and made a circle. *Please.*

"No, sweetheart," Sally said, curling her small and ring finger to her palm, and bringing her middle and ring fingers to the tip of her thumb. *No.* "One bowl is plenty."

Before long, Sarah was saying the words as she signed them.

———

I realized that Sally was right about the walker. It was dark outside, and the glass of the window next to the table reflected the kitchen light. She stared past her reflection to the arbor just outside the window, thorny with the dry vines of wild roses. I looked at her face. A fine sheen of tears had collected in her lower lids.

"The thing I said about the walker turning her into a cripple," I began.

She looked at me.

"Shitty thing to say." I folded my fingers together, knuckles out, to make a circular motion in front of my chest—the sign for *I'm sorry.*

"You're right." She watched my hand make the slow circles of contrition, and then looked to my eyes. "It was a shitty thing to say." Her voice sounded tired.

I looked from Sally to her dark reflection, and back to her. I was tired from being on call last night, and she was weary of staying home full-time with a special needs child, of having no backup every third night, sometimes every other. Of having a husband who was occasionally rattled, and chronically overwhelmed by his work at the hospital. A husband who came home depleted and stubborn. "It's hard," I said.

Sally rested her hand on the back of my neck. Her fingertips were cool, and made gentle soothing circles on my skin.

Sarah pulled herself up with the walker, and clutched the gray plastic handles molded onto the horizontal bars. She stood and swayed. Eventually, she walked from room to room. The walker became something she was hardly aware of: she seemed to carry it from force of habit—the metal legs clanging against furniture and door frames, and rarely touching the floor. It was no longer a symbol of Sarah's disability, it was just a thing—a set of training wheels.

Chapter Ten

"It's like an amniocentesis," Sally said, "only earlier. I won't even be showing." We were at the kitchen table, having a conversation we'd had before. Sally was ready to get pregnant again and wanted to quit taking birth control pills. Once pregnant, she planned to undergo chorionic villus sampling—a diagnostic procedure that could be done at eight to ten weeks gestational age—to make sure this one didn't have Down syndrome.

"I don't know about the chorionic villus sampling," I said. *Would we terminate a pregnancy because a prenatal test showed Down syndrome?*

It was 1990. Sarah was three years old, asleep in her crib upstairs. Sally leaned back in her chair. The table between us was empty, cleared of supper dishes. The incandescent light from the fixture in the ceiling formed stark shadows on Sally's face. She looked directly into my eyes, waiting for me to say more.

In decisions about our family, I'd always tended to trust Sally's judgment more than my own. When I met Sally, seven years previously, I'd already failed once at marriage: I'd gotten married in my mid-twenties, and after a couple of years my wife walked up the steps of a Greyhound bus and rode home to her parents. She said I was too intense and unyielding, wound too tightly. She was probably right. She had some issues of her own. I had always been glad that we hadn't had kids.

When Sally was pregnant with Sarah, she didn't undergo amniocentesis: based on her age—thirty-four—and the fact that the alpha-fetoprotein level was within the normal range, the possibility of accidentally inducing an abortion of a healthy fetus was greater than the likelihood of identifying a fetus with a problem. Alpha-fetoprotein—abbreviated AFP—is a molecule made in the liver of the fetus. The AFP passes through the placenta and into the maternal blood, where it can be measured. The level of AFP in Sally's blood was slightly elevated, but not above the threshold to suggest Down syndrome, or any other problem. Sally was confident that our baby was fine. She'd never smoked, she didn't drink while pregnant, and she exercised regularly. When the doctors talked with us about the AFP and her age, the odds were all in our favor.

―――

Sally ran her hand across the red and white checked table-cloth of the kitchen table, smoothing out wrinkles, and waiting for me to respond to her idea that we try again and this time, do definitive prenatal testing. I sat across from her. Sally's cat, River, jumped up into her lap. She rubbed River's head and stroked her hand down River's back. Waited.

Sally had an inviolate right to make her own decisions about her body. That was a given. But I wasn't sure that I wanted to help start a human life if we were going to end it.

"What would it mean about Sarah?" I asked.

She stared at me, with her jaw clenched. Lips thin. She was motionless. "She wouldn't need to know."

"Of course she wouldn't," I said. "But every time she smiles, or laughs, or needs to be changed, I'd wonder, would we have aborted her?"

―――

"I don't know," I said to Sally. "What if it turns out that a fetus *is* a tiny person?" It was dark outside, 10 pm, and I had to be back at the hospital at 6 am. Sally and I were in the bedroom, undressing. Sarah was asleep in the room across the hall.

"If I decided to get an abortion, it would be my decision," she said, stepping out of her panties. "You'd be off the hook." She pulled the covers down on her side of the bed and got in.

"But I'm already on the hook." I tossed my shirt and jeans on a chair next to the bed, took off my socks and underwear, and got into bed. Leaving Sally with Sarah would be so cowardly that I wouldn't even consider it

The fact was, I was firmly on the hook, and it's where I wanted to be. I wasn't some lout. I wanted to be there at the birth, and the grade school play, the skinned knees and stubbed toes and talking too much on the phone, college, grandkids. I was in it for keeps and I wanted to do the right thing.

"The chorionic villus sampling would probably be normal," Sally said. "We'd probably just sigh a big sigh of relief."

"But what if it shows Down syndrome?"

"We'll deal with it." She pulled the blankets up to her chin. "Either way, I'm ready to stop taking the pill."

"How was work?" Sally asked. We were sitting at the kitchen table, two days later, with the supper dishes pushed back. Sarah was asleep in her high chair, her head lolling against her left shoulder.

"Not bad," I said.

"I know you're tired," she said, "but we need to decide."

I waited.

"I don't see why you can't just let it happen," Sally said. "Get chorionic villus sampling."

"And if it shows trisomy?"

"If it shows trisomy," Sally said, enunciating each word with precision, "I will have an abortion."

"And if abortion is morally wrong?"

"Which is the greater 'moral wrong'? Aborting a first-trimester fetus, or forcing your wife to carry a defective child?" Her eyes filled with tears. "I don't think I could raise a second child with problems." Her voice sounded tired. Flat. "I don't think I'd survive." Sally had a long history of depression. She didn't talk about it much: partly due to stoicism, partly due to being very private, and partly due to using denial as a coping mechanism.

The cat meowed at the door.

Sally didn't move.

Sarah's head bobbed. She woke and began to cry.

Sally sighed, blotted her eyes with a napkin, and slowly stood.

"I can change her," I said, sliding my chair back.

"I've got it," Sally said, unclipping the high chair's belt around Sarah's waist. Sally's movements were slow and deliberate. She put Sarah on her shoulder and gently patted her back as she walked toward the stairs to Sarah's room.

Chapter Eleven

The tires of the station wagon thumped across the expansion joints of the bridge crossing the Ohio River. The steel beams above formed angular shadows that crisscrossed the pavement, making a syncopated strobe of the winter morning sun. "Sarah," I said, pointing through the windshield toward an Orthodox church. "Do you see the golden roofs?"

In the back seat, Sarah leaned forward against the straps securing her in her car seat, and squinted. She gave up and looked up at me in the rearview mirror. She must not have been able see over the front seat. We were heading for a different church, the Mother of Sorrows, for Sarah's Early Intervention class, a preschool for children with developmental delays, but I wished she could see the glints of sun from the gold bulbs rising above the trees. They looked like something in St. Petersburg or Moscow. I winked at her.

Sarah was five years old. She returned my wink by squinching both eyes. Her nose wrinkled and her mouth twisted. Sarah was able to raise both eyebrows to show surprise, or one eyebrow to express disbelief or to register irony, but she hadn't perfected her wink. She was working on it, though.

I was driving a dove-gray Buick station wagon my mother-in-law had given us when we moved to Pittsburgh. It had velour seats and power steering. The sides of the car were laminated with a plastic film that was meant to look like wood.

We turned down a steep and narrow street of two-story houses with aluminum awnings and close-trimmed shrubs. We passed a house with blue canvas lawn chairs leaning against a cinderblock foundation, and asphalt shingles crumbling at the edges of the roof. We pulled into the parking lot of the Saint Peter's Mother of Sorrows church, and got out of the car.

Sarah had a jaunty walk, as if she were eager to see what was next. I took her hand, and we walked across the street to the tan brick church. I didn't know what to expect, or where to go, but Sarah did; Sally had been bringing her here for a year.

Sarah led me to a classroom on a lower level, with a row of windows at the ceiling. The room had the feel of being halfway underground—a partial basement. The walls were cinderblock, painted a glossy white. The blinds were opened to bring in as much sun as possible, and light slanted downward across the floor.

Child-sized chairs formed a circle in the middle of the room. Sarah's classmates sat next to their moms, who sat with knees in the air, pocketbooks on the floor next to them. I smiled and nodded at the teacher and to each of the five mothers, careful not to stare at their kids, but also careful not to look away.

I couldn't help comparing Sarah to the other children, and at first glance, she had much more sparkle than any of the other children.

One boy didn't have a mom next to him. Must be Kevin, the child we were supposed to take home with us, so his mother could come by our house to pick him up that afternoon.

"Hello," I said to him. "Are you Kevin?"

His neck was twisted to the right, and downward, tucking his chin down almost to his collarbone. To look my way, he leaned his body back, and raised his eyebrows as far as he could. His forehead wrinkled with the effort, and his eyes bulged, giving him an expression of surprise, or pain. He looked at me, his head bobbing slightly.

"You must be Sarah's dad," the teacher said. "I'm Ms. Hines. Kevin's mom said that you'd be taking him home."

"Yup." I gave Kevin a thumbs-up. "Glad to give you a ride."

His head bobbed. I couldn't tell if it was a nod or a twitch.

Sarah sat beside me and looked at Ms. Hines, who was standing next to a felt board on a low, A-frame easel. I had a feeling she was ready to begin class, and that we might have been late. I snuck a look at my watch. Dead on 9 am.

"Good morning." Ms. Hines spoke clearly and distinctly. She smiled.

"Good morning," the mothers and I answered in a chorus that matched her tone. Sarah's response was just half a beat behind. Sarah had to try her best when she was talking, because her speech could be indistinct and difficult to understand. Her voice had a torque that I'd noticed in the speech of other children with Down syndrome. Not nasal exactly. Not thick-tongued. But there was a brogue, or a lilt or a slurring that became more prominent when she was tired or talking too fast.

Ms. Hines had long, delicate fingers. She held small patches of colored felt. Her movements were slow. Careful. Deliberate.

"Do we remember what we went over last week?" She looked at each child. "Our shapes and colors?"

Kevin, a few seats over, made a guttural sound. His neck muscles tightened and his mouth opened wide, and he twisted his head up and further to the right and shrieked. It was a loud, squawking sound, as if a sheet of tin was being torn loose from rusty nails.

I flinched at the sound, and then glanced around. No else seemed to notice the shriek. I was embarrassed at having been startled, but no one seemed to notice that, either.

Kevin's eyes widened as the shriek scaled up further, and then subsided. His muscles relaxed.

Ms. Hines paused for another moment, as if to make sure Kevin was through. She smiled at him and continued. "We have a green square." She held a piece of felt between her forefinger and thumb. She turned right, and left, to make sure everyone saw it. "And a red circle, a blue star, and a yellow triangle." She held each shape up in turn.

A girl sitting across from us was looking down at her hands in her lap. She also had Down syndrome. When she looked up, her face was slack, as if gravity had more effect on her expression than her nerves and muscles, as if inertia had more power than her thoughts and feelings. Her hair was thin and mousy brown. Her mouth was open and her tongue protruded slightly, just covering her lower lip.

I had an impulse to reach over and tap her tongue with my finger. When Sarah was just months old, a physical therapist told us that if we tapped Sarah's tongue every time we saw it hanging out, she'd quickly learn to keep it inside her mouth. It wasn't that the tongue was too big, the therapist told us; it was habit, or decreased muscle tone, that made the tongue protrude.

———

In the past, some experts advocated trimming the tongues of people with Down syndrome. I couldn't imagine cutting off part of Sarah's tongue. An article in a medical journal from the 1970s shows photographs and drawings of a nine-year-old girl with Down syndrome who had undergone six operations in the same day.[43] The epicanthal folds were removed. The slant of her eyes was corrected. The bridge of the nose was lifted with an insert. The tongue was made smaller. The receding chin was corrected with an insert. Fatty tissue under the chin was scraped away. A line drawing of the procedure on the tongue surgery shows a pie-shaped chunk cut away from the front of the tongue, leaving a huge V-shaped gap that will be drawn together and sewn. Like a dart or pleat.

In the "after" photographs, the girl was prettier. But when her parents pulled the bandages off to stare into the bruised face of their daughter, did she still look like herself?

There is no doubt that if Sarah were burned, we'd do skin grafts. If she'd been born with a cleft palate, we'd have the gap in her upper lip closed. But changing her eyes, or ears, or nose, would seem like we were trying to change her identity. How could we explain it to her? If there were a new technology that could remove the extra 21st chromosomes in each of Sarah's cells—if the Down syndrome could dis-appear and Sarah would be "just Sarah," rather than "Sarah who has Down syndrome"—I would do it.

That technology, however, did not exist. Sarah would always have Down syndrome. Her slanted eyes and low-set ears gave people a cue that she was different. Hopefully they'd cut her a little slack. And if Sally and I helped her enough with physical therapy, speech therapy, Early Inter-vention classes, she might not "pass" as "normal," but maybe she would be included by the rest of the world.

———

Ms. Hines repeated the shape and color as she placed each swatch on the felt board and smoothed it with her fingertips. "Did everybody see?" She reidentified each shape. "Do we remember?" The moms all nodded, almost imperceptibly.

"Bobby," Ms. Hines said. "Can you show me the red circle?"

A boy stood, his face serious, cheeks flushed. In his flan-nel shirt and jeans cuffed up at the bottom, he looked like a farmer looking over a large field he had to plow. He walked up to the easel and stared at the shapes. He slowly raised his right hand, and then let it drop back down. He paused again and then pointed. Red circle.

"Good!" Ms. Hines's voice scaled upward in praise. "You picked the red circle."

Bobby slowly walked back, his stride slow. Face serious. When he got back to his seat, he put his hands on his knees. His mother, a thin woman with deep-set eyes and pink snow boots, touched his arm and leaned down to say something.

He nodded.

"Kevin," the teacher said. "Can you show us the green square?"

Kevin's head bobbed, and he muffled a shriek. Maybe he had Tourette's syndrome. His facial features were symmetrical, normal, except for the wrinkled forehead and bulging eyes.

Kevin stood.

"The green square," Ms. Hines's voice was calm, encouraging.

Kevin leaned back at the waist to look at the easel.

"You know this," the teacher said. "You can do it."

The other kids looked from Kevin to the easel and back.

Ms. Hines gestured toward the felt board and nodded at Kevin.

He walked toward the easel, his body turned to the left, his head twisted to the right, gathering momentum, as if he'd lost his balance and was trying to catch up with himself. His right hand was extended, pointing at the board.

When he reached the board, he abruptly stopped, his hand pointing to the yellow triangle.

Ms. Hines gently deflected Kevin's hand down and to the left. "The green square," she said. "Good job. You're pointing to the green square."

Kevin gripped a corner of the square and peeled it from the board.

"Let's leave it here," Ms. Hines said, prying his fingers free. "We leave the shapes on the board."

He continued to clutch the green square.

"Kevin," the teacher said. "We leave the shapes on the board." She pulled harder, and the square slipped from between Kevin's fingers.

"Good," she said, as she turned Kevin toward his chair. "You can sit down now."

He walked back to his chair, his arms angled slightly out to the side, if walking across the deck of a moving ship, or back to his seat in an airplane that has just hit turbulence. The teacher held the green square, which had been pulled out of shape. She tugged on it from several directions, and then smoothed it back to the board. The edges were wavy, and it was skewed into a new shape.

"Sarah," Ms. Hines said as she turned to face the class again. "Can you show us the blue star?"

Sarah stood. She was wearing her favorite clothes: pink

corduroy pants and a white turtleneck. She walked to the board and without hesitation pointed to the blue star.

"Good, Sarah," the teacher said.

Sarah smiled as she walked back to her chair. After she sat, she let out a deep breath. She'd been nervous. I patted her leg, and then she patted mine.

The moms looked like average PTA or bake sale moms, sitting with their pocketbooks beside their feet, giving pats and hugs in encouragement or consolation.

Kevin's mom had left a car seat, a big, bulky plastic thing with checkered padding. I wrestled it into the back seat of the station wagon, jostled it, cinched down the seatbelt, jostled it again, cinched it down again.

"Okay, Kevin," I said, "in you go."

He reared back so he could look up at me.

I patted the car seat with the palm of my hand.

He lurched up into the car, and climbed into the car seat. He struggled as he threaded his arms though the straps in the seat, but eventually sat there, the straps over his shoulders, his chin tucked down against his collarbone.

As we crossed the Ohio River, Kevin screeched. It was

a squawking, birdlike sound, like a crow or a falcon would make.

In the rearview mirror, Sarah's eyes met mine. She raised her eyebrows and shrugged.

Kevin's body pulled against his seat belts, and then the screech began to wind down. The expansion joints of the bridge kept making their thumping sounds.

I looked in the rearview mirror again. Sarah winked by squinching her eyes at me. I winked back.

Chapter Twelve

"The results came back," Sally said.

I'd just gotten home, and was still holding the nylon gym bag I'd carried to the hospital the day previously, for my night on call—shaving kit, clean socks, clean underwear. I tried to keep my voice and face neutral. "And?"

"Normal." She stepped toward me.

I dropped my call bag on the kitchen table and spread my arms for a hug.

She put her cheek on my shoulder, and wrapped her arms around me. Her small frame felt solid.

I'd hoped to feel happy, or at least relieved, but I still felt as if my insides were being pulled downward. I was glad to know the results were normal—but so many things could still go wrong over the next seven months, and during delivery, and during the first few weeks of life. I kissed the top of Sally's head.

We lived a few blocks from the main street of Westview, a small township just north of Pittsburgh. We decided to walk to a local restaurant to celebrate, and took turns pushing Sarah's stroller. Cars were nosed into angled parking spaces in front of Westview Borough City Hall. We strolled past Isaly's Deli, and then further down the steep hill, to DiPietro's Ristorante.

We sat in a booth.

"I feel better," Sally said. She took a sip of ice water. "Knowing."

"Me too."

Sarah was in a child's seat, pulled close to the table. She looked from Sally to me, and back to Sally.

The waitress brought our salads. Wedges of iceberg lettuce, pale hard tomato slices. Thousand island dressing, thick and pink. Two packets of Captain's Wafer crackers. I tore off the cellophane and handed a cracker to Sarah.

She took it, turned her head sideways, and started chewing. She was three years old. Developmentally about two or three, depending on which test was performed.

"You okay?" Sally asked.

"Tired," I said.

Sally handed Sarah a sippy cup. Sarah casually put it to

her lips and took a sip. She put it on the table without spill-
ing a drop.

"Good job!" Sally and I said simultaneously. We then
laughed at having said the exact same thing.

Sarah laughed along, and then smiled at me, and then at
Sally. She finished her cracker.

We ate our salads. The pizza came, and I trimmed off a
wedge of crust and gave it to Sarah. She held it in her fat
little fist, and chewed. We talked about my night on call.
About Sally and Sarah's day.

On the walk back home, I asked if our new baby was a
boy or a girl.

"Boy," Sally said.

———

Sally's body changed with the second pregnancy in the
same ways it had with the first: her breasts and belly swelling, her gait developing an indolent sway. Making love, we
accommodated the new geometries of curve and angle with
the same adjustments we discovered the first time, but this
time we felt less adventuresome, and more tender.

———

The C-section went without a hitch, and we named the baby John.

"He has a faint heart murmur," the obstetrician told us in the recovery room.

Here we go. My belly muscles tightened.

Sally lifted her head from the pillow to look at the doctor. Her face was puffy and pale.

"I went ahead and ordered an echo," he said.

Sally kept her voice level. "Anything else?"

"Nope," he said. "Everything else looks good."

Sally rested her head on the pillow, and folded her hands over her chest with her fingers interlaced. She closed her eyes.

I pulled my chair closer to her bed.

Later that day Dr. Swenson, a cardiologist, came by the hospital room. Sally was resting with her eyes closed. "The echo's normal," the cardiologist whispered. "Thought you'd want to know as soon as possible."

"Thanks," I whispered back. "I'll tell Sally when she wakes up."

He gave me a thumbs-up, and left.

Sally opened her eyes. "I heard."

We took John home from the hospital, emptied a dresser drawer, padded it with folded bath towels, and used it for his bed. Over the previous months, I'd been looking at wood-working plans for cradles. I would enjoy using hand tools—saw, plane, and chisels—to shape the wood that would hold my sleeping son. I could adapt a Shaker design: something solid and simple in walnut or oak. John could someday rock his children in the same bed. But I hadn't made a cradle for Sarah—I didn't have access to a shop in married student housing—so we'd bought a crib. Sarah was still sleeping in it. In our house in Pittsburgh, I had a small shop in the base-ment. A cradle would be a great project: small, and simple, it would be easy to complete. But for something so straightfor-ward, the project seemed complicated. If I made it, it would become a family heirloom to pass down to future children. Children that John could have, but Sarah couldn't.

By the time John had outgrown his drawer, Sarah was able to sleep in a bed, and John moved into the store-bought crib.

When John was two years old and Sarah was six, Sally said she'd like to have a third child, followed by a tubal liga-tion. We didn't even discuss whether or not we'd do chorionic villus sampling. When she got pregnant, it came back normal.

I'd finished my residency training, and was junior faculty at the East Carolina University School of Medicine. Publishing papers, teaching residents. We bought a two-story frame house in an upper-middle-class neighborhood with tall pine trees and carefully mowed, very green yards.

Sam's C-section was routine, and he was healthy. When Sam was nine months old, we moved to Durham, North Carolina, where I was starting a new job in an ER. I was ready to be just a doc in an ER, instead of a professor of emergency medicine; I never learned how to say no to work, and at the university, between working my shifts on clinical duty in the ER and lectures, and meetings, and research projects, I could go twenty-five days in a row without taking a single day off. I was worn out, and just wanted to work my shifts and go home. I was ready to be free from worries about a career, about advancing up the hierarchy of academics.

Sally got a part-time job at the Duke University Chromosomal Clinic. She was a parent liaison between the clinicians and the families of the patients, most of whom had Down syndrome. She also stayed in contact with the genetics program at UNC in Chapel Hill, where Sarah was born.

Occasionally, medical students and pediatric residents from UNC who were interested in Down syndrome and other developmental delays came to our house for dinner to observe a family with a child with special needs.

"There's a couple that may want to come by," Sally said one evening. "They've got three kids, all girls, and are pregnant with a fourth. Down syndrome. Boy." Sam was two, John was four, and Sarah was eight.

I put down the magazine I'd been reading. "Who are they?"

"I don't know," Sally said. "Elaine asked if she could give the couple our name and phone number. He's an ER doc, she's a nurse."

"Huh," I said. "An ER doc and a nurse. Sure. I guess so."

Sally waited to see if I had more to say.

"Does it seem a little strange?" I asked. It was as if Sarah was a car they wanted to test-drive.

"Not really," Sally said, holding her place in her book. "And they may not even call. Elaine was just asking if she could give them our number, in case they do want to meet Sarah. But if you're not comfortable with it, I'll just tell her no."

Ten years later, in 2007, the American College of Obstetrics and Gynecology would make new recommendations: that prenatal testing for Down syndrome be offered to all women, regardless of age. Prior to these recommendations, only women thirty-five and older were routinely tested. Of the women whose tests identified a fetus with Down syndrome, 90 percent had an abortion.

The *New York Times* reported this in an article about a new movement in the Down syndrome community, in which families with a child with Down syndrome offer to meet with couples with a prenatal diagnosis of Down syndrome.

"The parent 'evangelists' are driven by a deep-seated fear for their children's well-being in a world where there are fewer people like them . . ." The article goes on to say:

> the richness of their children's lives, parent advocates say, is poorly understood. Early medical intervention and new expertise in infant heart surgery stave off many health problems; legally mandated inclusion in public schools has created opportunities for friendship and fostered broader social awareness of the condition.
>
> Many participants in the ad-hoc movement describe themselves as pro-choice. Yet some see themselves as society's first line of defense against a use of genetic technology that can border on eugenics. "For me, it's just faces disappearing," said a mother to four daughters including one with Down syndrome, "It isn't about abortion politics or religion, it's a pure ethical question." [44]

Even after reading it several times, I didn't quite understand the distinctions being made between abortion politics, and religion, and a purely ethical question.

But in 1997, Sally and I were not part of a movement. We were just parents of a daughter with Down syndrome, and we'd heard about a couple facing a difficult decision. If having a beer and a burger with them would help, why not?

———

Their van pulled up at 5:02. Our house was on a corner lot in a tree-shaded neighborhood built in the 1920s. The side street, just half a block long, had never been paved. The sides of the ditch between our yard and the gravel of the road had a fairly steep slope.

James pulled their van into the side street with the passenger side wheels right at the edge of the ditch. Sally and I walked out to greet them.

Sally, James, Elise, and I all shook hands.

The girls clustered behind their mother's legs.

"Why so shy all of a sudden?" Elise said. She stepped aside and introduced each of the girls. They were three, five, and seven.

"There's a playhouse out back," I said, "and a dogwood tree that's great for climbing."

The girls looked up at their mom. "Let's go see it," she said.

"We'll go through the house," Sally said, "grab the Austin kids."

James and I followed.

Five days after the article in the *New York Times*, Eunice Kennedy Shriver, the founder of Special Olympics, wrote an article for *America: The National Catholic Weekly* about the American College of Obstetrics and Gynecology's recommendations that all pregnant women be offered prenatal testing for Down syndrome. "When Down syndrome is identified during pregnancy, however, the pregnancy termination rate grows to an estimated 90 percent, which leaves those of us who know and work with children with Down syndrome outraged about the effects of prenatal testing."[45]

John, six, and Sam, four, climbed the lower branches of an old, gnarled dogwood tree, glancing from time to time at the three girls, who were in the playhouse. I had built it a couple of years previously. It was four feet wide, eight feet long, and eight feet high, with large cutouts for the windows and door. One of the girls looked out of a window. She was wearing a red plastic fireman's hat.

"Where's Sarah?" I asked Sally.

"She's in her room, coloring," Sally said. "She'll be down later."

James and Elise smiled at each other, and then at us. They'd driven an hour and a half to get to our house, and I imagined they were eager to meet Sarah.

The four of us sat in lawn chairs, sipping Corona beer. James and I talked about the emergency departments we worked in. His ER saw 55,000 patients a year, mine saw 50,000. About the same mix of trauma and medicine, pediatric and adult.

Sally took Elise inside for a tour of the house, and later returned with Sarah.

"Show James your drawings," Sally said.

Sarah handed him the piece of paper.

"Who is it?"

"Snow White," she answered. "With the dwarves."

"Who?" James said, leaning forward, smiling.

"Snow White. And the dwarves."

James glanced up at me.

"Snow White?" I said to Sarah, looking at the drawing in James's hand. "And the dwarves?"

Sarah nodded.

"That's who I thought it was," James said. "Very good."

"Thanks." Sarah looked over at Sam and John standing side by side on a limb of the dogwood tree, and then to the playhouse.

"Would you like to meet my girls?" Elise said.

"That's okay," Sarah said. She sat on Sally's lap.

"Sarah draws a lot," Sally said.

"Our girls like to draw, too," Elise said.

"What's for supper?" Sarah asked.

"Big-Daddy special hamburgers," I said.

"Oh, brother." Sarah rolled her eyes. "Here we go again." She looked over to Elise. "My dad's a big jokester."

Elise and James chuckled.

"Can I go back and draw?" Sarah asked Sally.

Sarah looked at her brothers in the dogwood tree again, and at the girls in the playhouse, and then went back inside.

"Her drawings have so many details," Elise said.

The people in Sarah's drawings tended to be tall, thin, and made almost exclusively of elongated ovals. Snow White was holding a large, round red apple. The dwarves were all skinny, about half as tall as Snow White. The elves had hats, and pointy shoes that curled up at the toes.

"She can be shy," I said, wishing she'd wanted to play with the other kids. "But that's okay with us. One of the stereotypes is that 'children with Down syndrome love everybody.' We aren't against love or anything, but we're glad she doesn't run up and hug random strangers."

"She seems mature," James said. "Engaging."

"Our OB doc told us she'd be more like other kids than unlike them," I said. "It's been true in Sarah's case. She's a good kid. But the Down syndrome has put some stress on the family."

"I guess all kids do," James said.

———

The *New York Times* article didn't mention the legal risk an obstetrician runs by not offering prenatal testing. In June 2007, in the journal *Clinics in Perinatology,* two attorney/physicians wrote, "The usual claim against a physician or other provider is not that of causing damage or disease in the fetus but of causing a loss of opportunity to prevent conception or live birth of an infant who has an abnormality."[46]

———

Like most parents of children with disabilities, I will always be grateful to Eunice Kennedy Shriver for starting Special Olympics. She gave us the chance to watch our children run and play, without the wincing fear that someone will laugh at their awkwardness or slow reflexes. Special Olympics brought our children out into the sun.

But after reading her article on the issues of prenatal testing, I didn't feel the outrage she wrote about. What I felt was more of an ache.

———

Sally and I walked Elise, James, and their kids to the van. After everyone was seatbelted in, James started the van and put it in gear. The back tire at the edge of the ditch spun, cutting through the thatch of grass and into red clay underneath. He backed up and tried again. More spinning, grass and red mud spraying backward from underneath the tire.

"I can give you a pull," I said, pointing to my pickup truck. "Wouldn't take a second."

He rolled down his window. "I think I can make it." The tire spun and the van slowly moved forward until the tires made it up to the gravel.

———

"They seemed nice enough," I said as I rinsed a plate and put it the dishwasher.

"They've got a lot on their minds." Sally stretched a piece of clear plastic wrap over a plate of tomato slices.

"Do they think they're going to keep it?"

"She's thinking not."

"What's he thinking?" I rinsed a plate.

"He really wants a son," Sally said, "and it's a boy."

"Hard decision," I said.

"She's concerned that he doesn't have a realistic idea of what a child with Down syndrome would involve."

"Seemed realistic enough."

"He has some depression," Sally said, closing the refrigerator door. "She doesn't think he'd do well."

I walked out into the side yard and looked at the long red gash down the side of the ditch. The rut was four inches deep, and the edge had a ridge about three inches tall. I pressed my foot down on the edge, feeling it give under my weight, and thought about getting a shovel to try to smooth it all out.

Chapter Thirteen

Sarah's disabilities sometimes made interactions clumsy. Conversations at mealtime were difficult. Our rectangular oak kitchen table was pushed against the wall, and I sat at one end, Sally at the other. The kids sat on the long side— John at my end, Sarah at Sally's end, and Sam in the middle.

If John mentioned something about his second-period English class, Sarah would interrupt to say that it reminded her of a scene in a movie. Sally or I would tell Sarah that we wanted to hear what she had to say, but that she needed to wait until John was finished talking. Sarah would fold her arms tightly across her chest and slump in her chair, her bottom lip protruding. John would start over, directing his attention to Sally or me, sometimes to Sam. Sarah would sit immobile, staring at her plate. John would tell us about his English class, but the sparkle in his voice would be muted by Sarah's angry presence. It seemed that telling us about his day had become work: like trudging through waist-high snow.

Once John had told his story, and Sally and I had

responded, Sarah would say, "*Now* can I talk?" She would then lean forward and tell us about a scene in a movie.

If she made a special effort with her diction, we could understand most of what she said. But if she spoke too quickly, or wasn't careful, she produced a stream of sound that carried only occasional words that could be recognized.

After talking for several minutes, Sarah would look at each of us to see if we'd understood. Her brothers always understood her better than Sally or I did, but they often found it easier to nod, eat, and pretend to listen. So did I, mirroring Sarah's facial expressions as closely as I could. Sarah would sense that I wasn't understanding her, so she'd turn to Sally and repeat herself: "What I *said*, was . . ." Sally was too kind, or too loving, or too attached, to ignore her. So Sally would carefully put her fork down on her plate, and say, "Speak slowly and clearly so we can understand you."

Sarah would lean back in her chair, cross her arms again, and frown. Sally or I would try to pick up an earlier thread of conversation, and then Sarah would unfold her arms and sit up straight, and start talking again, forming each word as meticulously as she wrote, her fingers scrunched up at the end of her fat pencil, her shoulders hunched forward, her lower lip caught between her teeth, trying to keep misshapen letters between the wide lines of her practice paper.

On the other hand, Sarah was bright and social. She never had tantrums, or bit herself or others. She never had seizures, or needed to be fed after infancy. From the time she was eight, she was able to wash her own hands, brush her teeth, and brush her hair. But we had to teach her these skills over and over. It became a daily catechism we practiced for years: Brush your teeth. Wash your face. Brush your hair. I mimed each activity: lips drawn back, hand jiggling beside my mouth, cupping imaginary water to splash against my face, and, finally, my hand smoothing hair that I pretended went to my shoulders.

When the school system first tested her IQ, she scored one point too high to be classified as "mentally retarded," so she didn't qualify for special education. On the other hand, given what the schools had to offer, she could never have kept up in a regular classroom. She was designated "other health impaired," by virtue of her Down syndrome, so she could get some individual attention from the special needs teacher.

With a calm, clear voice, the teacher explained to Sally and me that although Sarah's IQ was encouraging, it would slip downward with subsequent testing; the later tests concentrate on more abstract thinking, and Sarah's strengths would be in the concrete. The teacher was right: over the years, Sarah's number dropped slowly, until she was near the top of her intellectually disabled peers but a clear division away from the regular kids. If she tried her best she might eventually get into a good group home—one that would offer friendship, support, and as much independence as possible.

Chapter Fourteen

We had a family membership at the "new" YMCA in down-town Durham, and enjoyed the juice bar in the lobby and the aquatics center, with its two huge pools and ceramic tile hot tub. There were steam rooms, and saunas, and child-care. I had never visited the "old" Y, until I went to watch Sarah compete in Special Olympics. It was a block away from a once busy strip mall, where dark windows faced an empty asphalt parking lot tufted with clumps of grass struggling through the cracks. At one end of the long low building, a Salvation Army Store had opened. Next door, a storefront tabernacle had closed.

On a drizzly Saturday morning I was standing in the gym of the old Y with the other parents. Sally and I were waiting for Sarah to do her routine. The windows were way up near the ceiling. Small and dusty, they gave a faint amber glow. The air had a subtle, pungent smell of stale sweat and a dry, autumnal smell of heating ducts. An astringent note of chlorine floated in from the small, tile-lined pool that was down the hall. John and Sam had gone to the other gym, to watch a pickup game of basketball.

In any competition, someone wins and someone loses; that's why they keep score. In Special Olympics, the judges have stopwatches and scorecards, pens and paper. Everything is carefully tallied and recorded. But care is taken that there are no "losers." The participants are carefully grouped by age and ability, and the lowest score in a given event has to be within 10 percent of the highest. Since athletes are grouped by ability, everyone competes against people with similar capabilities. In basketball, for instance, an athlete who couldn't compete in an actual game can compete on individual skills: target pass, 10-meter dribble, and spot shot.

Everyone gets a ribbon or a medal, and everyone gets a chance to stand on the podium. Most of the athletes understand that a medal is better than a ribbon, and that gold is better than silver, which is better than bronze. Many of them keep meticulous track of their standing in the competition—how many pounds they can deadlift, their best time on the 100-meter backstroke.

Good sportsmanship is stressed, and it's rare for a gold-medal winner to lord it over a competitor who was given a ribbon instead of a medal, but it sometimes happens— it's human nature. Some of the local athletes will advance to regional and state competitions. Some may go to the national competition, or even all the way to the world games.

Sarah had never been that competitive, and didn't seem to care much if she won or lost. And it didn't matter that much to Sally, or me. We were there to have fun.

A small-framed woman standing next to me asked, "Which one's yours?" She had fine dark hair pulled back in a yellow scrunchy. I recognized her but couldn't remember her name. We must have met at Special Olympics last spring.

Sally, who was talking to two other moms a few feet away, knew all the kids' names, and the names of their moms and dads. Siblings, too. After an event, she'd refer to someone's kid by name, and I'd stare at her with a blank expression, and she'd say, "You know her. The one with the two long braids down her back. And the crutches that fit around her arms." Sally would clamp her hand around her forearm to demonstrate. "Oh," I'd say. "Her." Sally would then go on to tell me how her mom had to write a letter to the school system, to make them provide a physical therapist.

"Sarah," I said to the woman next to me. "She's the next one up." With my chin, I gestured toward my daughter. "Yours?"

"Marybeth. She just went." The woman smiled toward a gangly girl sitting on a folding chair, her feet on the crossbar, her knees prominent, bony. There was nothing that looked dramatically wrong with her, but her neck extended just a little too far, and her ears were just a little too high. She sat with her mouth open. She didn't talk with the girl next to her, or watch the other contestants.

"She did great," I said. After her event, each of the three judges sitting behind a long table had held up a card: 6, 7, 7. I hadn't been to enough events to know if that was a high score or a low one. Marybeth didn't have Down syndrome or cerebral palsy. No other syndrome I could recognize. During her routine, she'd moved slowly, as if she'd been overmedicated; she had done all of the moves precisely, but with the same indifference with which she sat with her hands in her lap. After her routine, she sat with her face turned slightly upward, as if watching dust moving slowly in the air. I wondered what had gone wrong.

"How old is she?" I asked.

"Nineteen."

I nodded, and watched the child who was going before Sarah. Like Sarah, this girl had Down syndrome, but her face was less animated, and her body movements slower. She had rounded shoulders, a wide, pear-shaped body, and large fleshy thighs. Sparse bangs spread across her placid, unwrinkled forehead. She lifted a large red rubber ball and lowered it, without any apparent anxiety that she might mess up, and no excitement that her mom and dad, younger sister, and grandparents were there to watch her. She tossed the ball in the air, maybe two or three inches. Caught it. She gave a workmanlike performance, plodding though her moves.

"How long has Marybeth been doing Special Olympics?" The music stopped, but the young woman continued her routine, her breathing audible.

"Since she was ten," she said, without turning.

I nodded again. "Sarah's been doing it a couple of years. She's eleven."

"She's a cutie."

"Thanks." The heavyset child tossed the ball and caught it one last time. We were lucky Sarah hadn't gained a lot of weight.

The girl waited for her score: 6, 7, 6.

"Does Marybeth live with you?"

"We've been looking at group homes." She turned to look at me. "And we've thought about starting one. My husband's a contractor. He could adapt a house in the neighborhood. Find a few other families that could go in on it."

"Sally and I have talked about that too," I said, "but she thinks it would be hard, hiring staff, working out the benefits, salaries."

The other mom nodded. "Still, you'd know things were being done right."

I nodded.

"Of course, we've not done anything so far," the mom said. "Except talk about it."

"We've got Sarah on a waiting list," I said. "Over in Chapel Hill."

"RSI?" she said. "We've heard good things about them."

"The group home we visited was nice," I said. I was pretty sure we were talking about the same outfit. It had been a couple of years. Sally would know.

"Sarah's eleven?"

"We heard it could take years for a name to make it to the top of the list, so we went ahead and put her name in. If she's not ready when her name comes up, her name just floats up there near the top. We figure she'll move when she finishes high school. Her brothers will be going on to college, and we anticipate that she'll probably be ready to move on, too."

"How's Sarah doing in school?"

"She's in a self-contained classroom, but takes art and gym with the regular kids." Admitting that our daughter spends most of her day in a special education class, instead of full inclusion with other kids, made me feel as if I'd failed, especially when talking to another special needs parent.

Some parents insisted that their kid be included in regular-kid classes, and that the school provide an "inclusion assistant," a full-time person to help their child keep up. The problem was that there weren't enough inclusion assistants to go around. And I felt as if Sarah was already getting a lot of extra help from occupational therapists, physical therapists, speech therapists, and special education teachers. To threaten a lawsuit against the local school system, forcing them to pay someone to stay one on one with my child, seemed unreasonable. And I really didn't think Sarah would do that much better in a regular-kid class, even with someone sitting beside her, whispering encouragement and explaining assignments.

She needed to continue working on her basics. Simple math and reading. She could read a "chapter book," cover to cover, one word at a time, sounding out new words, reading the words she knew with fluency. It sounded as if she was actually reading. But if you stopped her after one page and asked her what it was about, she didn't know. I didn't think that sitting in the back of a classroom of regular kids would make her read better, or feel better. Or get along better. But maybe I was just rationalizing.

"Same with Marybeth." Her voice sounded tired. "She's in an EMH class, but a lot of the other students seem more EBD." There are a lot of acronyms to learn in the special needs community: TMH meant "trainable mentally handicapped," and in those classes students worked on life skills:

dressing themselves, eating with a spoon, tying their shoes. EMH meant "educable mentally handicapped," and in those classes they learned academic subjects: math and writing. EBD meant "emotional–behavioral disabled"—I knew there were specific criteria for EBD, but the EBD students seemed like regular kids who were too disruptive, needy, or noisy to be in with other students.

When I'd visited Sarah's special education class, most of the students seemed placid, earnest, and intellectually disabled. Other children looked normal but needy, intrusive and kinetic. Sarah tried to show me her daily journal, with its carefully penciled misspelled words, and drawings of princesses with dots for eyes, small noses, and oversized hands with five bulbous fingers. Some normal-looking kid came over, grabbed my hand, and insisted that I look at his finger painting.

Parents of EBD kids have complained that their kids are stigmatized by being put in classes with kids like mine. Parents of EMH kids wish the EBD kids wouldn't use up so much of the teacher's time.

"We've been having some problems," the mom said.

"Oh?" I didn't know if it was because we'd been lucky or if we'd just been too easily satisfied, but Sally and I hadn't had many problems with the Durham Public Schools. The school system was required to have an IEP—an Individual

Education Plan—for each child with special needs. A committee met twice a year, to list goals and objectives. "By the end of the term Sarah will be able to add and subtract sums up to 100." Or, "By the end of the term Sarah will be able to write a simple sentence, with no more than two spelling mistakes." Once she'd met all of the objectives, another set would be written.

When Sarah was eight years old, her physical therapist told us that she didn't need PT any more: she walked up and down stairs without holding a handrail, and managed all of the physical tasks required to go to school. We took it as a good sign, that she'd progressed, rather than as evidence that the school system was withdrawing services or shortchanging our daughter.

"Marybeth has been getting over-affectionate."

"Over-affectionate?"

"Oh, yes." The other mom turned to face me, eyebrows up, a wry smile on her face. "Once puberty hit, it was 'Katie bar the door.'"

"Yikes," I said, looking over at the lanky teenager, now sitting with her feet in her chair, her arms around her skinny knees.

"Yeah, no kidding." The mom shook her head. "Her teacher called us last week. And at home, she's been talking about sex. A lot."

———

Sally walked over. "Sarah's up next." Sally made an "eek" expression and hunched her shoulders, in play-nervousness.

I smiled back. No one in our family was that competitive about sports, but I knew Sarah would do better than 6, 7, 7. She'd get at least an 8 and a couple of 9's.

Stepping onto the mat, Sarah had the proud and jaunty walk of gymnasts on TV. In her leotard—blue and red, with white trim—she looked confident and poised. She stood in front of the judges' table, her head tilted just half a degree, as she waited.

The music started, and Sarah stood a bit straighter and then, holding the red rubber ball in both hands, she raised it above her head and swept her arms to the right, making a slow circle, like the hands of a clock. She stopped with the ball in front of her chest. Her elbows were sticking out to the sides. I didn't know if they were supposed to be, or not. She took three large steps forward, and stood for a moment with her feet together. She then extended her arms, holding the ball straight out in front, and took three steps backward.

Sarah was moving quickly. Her coach held her arms out, palms down, making a "slow down" motion. Sarah tossed the ball about a foot in the air, and caught it and pulled it to her chest. She then held her arms straight out and lowered them, letting the ball roll from her chest down to her hands. There was a brisk efficiency to each of her movements, and she seemed to be enjoying herself. At the end of the routine, she extended her right leg, and held the pose. The music continued on for two more beats, then stopped.

"Wow," the other mom said as we all started clapping. "She did great."

I waved at Sarah, who smiled but didn't wave back. "She did, didn't she?" I said.

Sarah stood in front of the judges' folding table and waited for them to lean over, make notations on a spiral-ring notebook, and then flip the white cardboard squares over, showing her score: 7, 7, 7.

I looked over at Sally, and then back at the numbers. That was at least a 9, 8, 8, or at worst, an 8, 8, 8. But Sarah seemed happy enough with her score, and Sally seemed pleased. I thought it was better than a 7, 7, 7. Way better.

Sarah walked over to where her team was sitting. Her shoulders were back and her chin up, as if still performing. She smiled at Clarisse, a tall African American girl with her hair brushed back into a blue hairband. Clarisse clapped her hands and shouted, "Go, Sarah!" Clarisse was Sarah's best friend. She had dark, wide-set eyes and a quick smile. There was just a little something "off" in the tone of her voice and the cadence of her speech, but she was outgoing and had a wry sense of humor.

Sarah sat cross-legged, and Clarisse patted her on the back. I was glad to see that Sarah's friends were on the less impaired end of the spectrum, rather than the profoundly so. Sarah was polite to all of her peers and clapped when her more disabled teammates walked up to stand in front of the judges' table. But just like the popular kids when I was at Ferndale Junior High, Sarah seemed to have an ease and confidence about her standing in her group.

In each of her events, she did better than some, not as well as others.

———

The awards banquet was covered-dish: paper plates, quart bottles of soda, and takeout boxes of fried chicken from several different fast food chains. I noticed a couple of classic standbys: string bean casseroles with onion-flavored snacks sprinkled across the top, macaroni and cheese.

Sarah's name was called, and she stepped up onto the platform without looking right or left. She ducked her head, her facial expression solemn, as her coach draped a ribbon around her neck. When she stepped down, she looked to her mom and me. She grinned and gave us a quick, excited wave. By the time it was over, she had two blue ribbons and one red, four certificates, and two medals.

I turned toward Sally, who was talking with a mom next to her. They were talking about Sibling Support Group, a monthly program for the siblings of children with special needs who met in a church meeting hall and ate pizza. They were supposed to share their feelings about having a sibling who was intellectually disabled.

"I have to force Roger and Elizabeth go," the other mom was saying.

"Same with Sam and John," Sally said. She turned to me and patted my leg. "Getting bored?"

"No," I said. "Yes. "

Sally and her friend laughed.

"Boys," the other mom said with an exaggerated roll of her eyes. They laughed again.

All these moms working so hard, I thought. All this energy to give all of their kids the best shot they can.

I had no idea how to be a Special Olympics dad.

Sarah walked over to where Sally and I sat. She had changed into a white top and pink knit pants.

"Let me see," I said, gesturing toward her medals.

"Mom first," Sarah said, laughing loudly.

I chuckled, not sure I got the joke.

Sarah handed a silver medal to her mother. "Ladies first," she said to me. "It's polite."

"Oh," I said. "My mistake."

"Yeah, yeah," Sarah said. "Always in a hurry." She handed the bronze medal to me. It felt light in my hand. "Good job," I said to Sarah, holding my arm out for a hug.

Sarah moved closer and leaned against me. "You ready to go home?" she asked.

"In a minute," I said. "Let me savor the moment. Bask in your glory."

"Yeah, right." She pulled away and looked at me, and smiled. She reached for her ribbons and medals. "I'll put them on my bulletin board up in my room. I've got some thumbtacks."

As I pulled out of the old Y's parking lot, Sally and Sarah chatted about her performance, and the other contestants and their families. They continued to talk as we drove past the half-empty mall, with its still-vacant lot.

PART TWO

Chapter Fifteen

"Sarah, you want to go to the Y with me?"

She was holding a royal blue crayon just above a page of typing paper. "I'm drawing." She didn't look up.

"After you finish your drawing?"

She looked over at me in my gym shorts and T-shirt.

"You can get on the rowing machine, or the bicycle," I said. "Come on. Father–daughter time. It'll be fun."

"Oh, brother. Here we go again." She rolled her eyes, dropped the crayon. "I'll finish it later."

I'd been going to the Y for about a year. In a fit of optimism, I had purchased a family membership. But John and Sam didn't like going with me, and with my rotating shifts, Sally and I rarely found a time that was convenient to go together. I began to encourage Sarah to go with me. Obesity is common in people with Down syndrome, as Taylor, a genetic counselor, had told me early on.

Taylor and I had known each other for a couple of years before Sarah was born: she'd been my tutor for genetics in my second year of medical school. Taylor and I both tended to be blunt and plainspoken. After Sarah was born, Taylor was our genetic counselor. As our session was winding up, Taylor paused. "One last thing: don't spoil her or let her get fat," she said. "No one likes a fat, spoiled retarded kid."

Although Sarah tended to stay in pretty good shape, when she was sixteen, Sally and I both noticed that she was getting a little big in the haunches.

"I'm glad you're going with me to work out," I told Sarah. "Keeps me motivated too."

Sarah nodded.

"And we need to make sure that you don't get overweight," I said. "Keep in shape."

"I get it," she said. "I get it."

———

Sarah was wearing a Little Mermaid T-shirt and big, baggy gym shorts. Two fitness instructors were showing her how the rowing machine worked. The instructors were in their mid-twenties. Fit and cheerful, one had a ponytail, the other short-cropped blond hair. They both wore YMCA shirts, stretched tight across the chest, tucked into the small waistbands of their shorts.

"I wasn't going to come," Sarah said in a loud voice, "but my dad talked me into it."

I was on an elliptical trainer, one row back from the rowing machines.

The trainer with the ponytail glanced back at me, and smiled. I smiled back, stood a little straighter as I bobbed up and down with the machine.

Sarah pulled on the handle of the rowing machine.

"Good job," the one with the short, feathered hair said, and then looked back at me to see if I was watching how well Sarah was doing.

We smiled at each other.

Sarah scooted her butt forward, allowing the machine to rewind. "You're getting it!!!" the one with the ponytail said.

A heavyset elderly woman sitting motionless on a nearby stationary bike watched.

Sarah pulled back again on the handles, and her machine made a faint whirring sound. "Fitness is important," Sarah said, pitching her voice above the sounds of the gym. "My daddy exercises a lot."

"Exercise *is* important," the one with the ponytail said. "I bet your father's proud of you." She smiled at me, and then at Sarah.

My chest swelled slightly. Such a good dad.

"He thinks I'm fat," Sarah said, her voice loud and matter-of-fact. The last word hung in the air.

The two trainers snapped their heads around to glare at me. *What an asshole.*

I flinched. *That's not what I said*. My legs lost their stride on the elliptical trainer, and I had to catch myself with the handrails.

The trainers turned their backs to me, and patted Sarah's shoulder.

———

Driving home, I looked over at Sarah.

"What?" she asked.

"The thing you said to the exercise instructors," I said.

"What thing?"

"When you told them I thought you're overweight." I said.

"I didn't say 'overweight,'" Sarah said. "I said 'fat.'"

Yes, I know. "I don't think you're fat," I said.

We rode silently.

"Exercise is good, whether you're overweight or not."

"I know, Dad, I know." She shook her head. "Sheesh."

Chapter Sixteen

Through the front door of the house, I heard music blaring. The volume was turned up so loud that it distorted the sound to the point that I couldn't identify the tune. Sarah, seventeen, was listening to one of her tapes in the radio/cassette player that Sally and I listened to while we cooked supper or loaded the dishwasher. At a normal volume it had plenty of depth and clarity, but Sarah had cranked it up so loud that the one small speaker rattled and buzzed as if it were tearing itself in half.

Sarah sat in a kitchen chair, weaving back and forth to a jingle-like melody. In front of her, an open quart of vanilla ice cream lay on its side, a glob of melting ice cream oozing onto the table. A jar of Nestle's Quik was open, and the dry brown powder had settled on the tabletop, chairs, and floor. The melted ice cream seeped into the pale brown dust and made it glisten, dark as espresso beans.

Sarah's eyes were closed, and her face was turned upward as she sang: "How do you solve a problem like Maria, how do you keep a wave upon the sand?" Her arms spread wide, palms up, fingers splayed.

It was a track from *The Sound of Music*—Sarah's favorite album. I had heard it a thousand times, Sarah's voice warbling half a beat behind. She had watched the video of the film so many times that a white grainy line skittered along the bottom of the screen. "She'd outpester any pest, drive a hornet from its nest, she could throw a whirling dervish out of whirl," Sarah sang along.

With her eyes still closed, Sarah swayed side to side. Strands of her blond hair had fallen into the bowl of soupy brown ice cream in front of her. The tips of her hair were matted into dark, sticky points.

I walked over to the tape player. Bits of pecans and chocolate chips crunched underfoot. I jabbed the "off" button with my finger.

Sarah jumped in her chair, and turned to look at me, eyes wide, mouth open. Her lips, cheeks, and forehead smeared with chocolate.

"What the hell are you doing?" I said, more baffled than angry. Sarah was typically so neat and orderly, so careful not to make a mess.

She stared at me. Then, in a soft, clear voice, she said, "Being wild."

I was too surprised to laugh.

The room was quiet. The afternoon sun streamed through the curtains, catching the fine brown dust floating in the air.

I felt a subtle pressure expanding in my chest. I didn't know what it was: maybe unexpected pride that she could be so articulate, so precise.

Outside, a lawnmower's drone was barely audible.

Sarah stared at me, waiting.

When I was seventeen, being wild involved the touch of clumsy, eager fingers. The taste of my girlfriend's tongue. A final, goodnight kiss in the front seat of the car. Then racing home through dark, winding roads, rural mailboxes flashing past in the headlights, bright and sharp-edged at the very moment they disappeared. The radio throbbing with AM rock and roll, and the night wind roaring through the open windows of my mother's Skylark coupe.

———

Ever since infancy Sarah had endured sessions with speech therapists, physical therapists, and occupational therapists. Special education classes. Inclusion with the normal kids. Mainstreaming. Relentless requests from her parents to "Make sure you speak slowly and clearly so we can understand you." Struggles to tie her shoes, make her bed, brush her teeth. Each skill had been an effort. Down syndrome had been her full-time job. It wasn't surprising that she wanted to bust loose. Be wild.

Melted ice cream dripped to the floor.

"Am I in trouble?" Sarah held my gaze.

"Look at this mess." My voice was stern.

Sarah leaned forward and looked at the floor.

"Pecans everywhere. Chocolate everywhere," I said. "What do you plan to do?"

"Clean it up?" she said.

"Yes ma'am."

She turned to look at the tabletop. "This too?"

"Of course."

She surveyed the mess on the floor and table. She seemed to have a sense of awe, maybe pride, at the extent of the wreckage she'd created.

"Do you want the music back on?" I asked.

I dialed the volume knob back down to a setting more suitable for news or classical music, and held my finger above the "play" button.

"No." She pushed away from the table. "The song was almost over."

Chapter Seventeen

Although she was as small as the children going house to house in costumes chosen by their mothers—Tinker Bell wings and leafy green leotards, or a plastic fire chief's helmet and a black coat with reflective trim—Sarah felt too old for trick or treating when she turned eighteen. She'd outgrown the pointed witch's hat, the American Girl costume.

Sam, fourteen, dressed up as Gene Simmons, the long-tongued bassist for KISS, and John, sixteen, went out without a costume.

I walked into the living room with a wooden bowl full of Snickers and Butterfingers, small yellow boxes of Dots, and white boxes of Junior Mints, with their subtle scent of mint and dark chocolate.

Sarah was lying on the bare oak floor in a white nightgown. Her hair was in French braids, and she wore ruby-red lipstick. Her hands were together over her belly, holding an apple.

I asked her what she was doing.

She answered, but I couldn't understand her.

"Can you say it again?" I asked. "Say each word carefully."

"For the kids," she said, pointing toward the front door, just a few feet away. "For Halloween." She turned her face toward the ceiling and closed her eyes. Her breathing was slow.

"Are you going to hand out candy?"

She opened her eyes and said a word that I couldn't make out.

I waited.

"A tableau," she said, enunciating carefully. She gestured toward the front door again. "For the kids to look at."

Ahh. "Want a pillow?" *Where does she get words like "tableau"?*

She lifted her head from the floor to shake it.

"Cinderella had a pillow."

"Snow White," Sarah said, resting her head again on the floor.

"She had one too."

Sarah closed her eyes again, her head shaking just a fraction.

I put the wooden bowl on a shelf next to the front door. "Do you want me to take a bite out of the apple? So it would look like Snow White bit the apple and then passed out?"

Sarah opened her eyes again. Frowned. "No." She closed her eyes. "But thanks."

I went back to the kitchen, started clearing supper dishes from the table.

The doorbell rang. It wasn't even dark out. Through the glass front door I saw a girl dressed in a puffy orange tunic with a collar of pale green leaves, standing with her mother. On the front of the girl's dress were two black triangular eyes, a triangle nose, and a gap-toothed grin.

"Happy Halloween," I said as I opened the door. Cold air rushed in.

The little girl looked at Sarah, lying on the floor, feet together, legs straight. The girl looked up at her mother's face, then back at Sarah.

"Is that Snow White?" I asked, to give the child a context for my daughter on the floor.

The child took a small step back.

"Is she under a spell? Waiting for a prince?"

The mom smiled at me. It was a crooked smile, and I couldn't tell if it was in appreciation of our little show, or if she could tell Sarah had Down syndrome, or if she was wishing we'd give her kid the damn candy so they could move on.

The child stared at Sarah.

I leaned down and held out the bowl.

The girl stared into the bowl, and took a box of Dots.

"Take another one," I said.

She paused, and took a Snickers bar.

"Say thank you," her mother said.

"Thank you," the girl said. She was staring at my daughter. She dropped the candy into her bag and looked at her mother, who placed a hand on her shoulder to turn her around.

Through the glass of the front door, I saw the child looking up at her mother's face. The child said something. The mother replied. The child took the mother's hand, and they walked toward the house next door.

"Dad," Sarah said. "You don't have to talk."

———

A year later, Sarah, nineteen, decided to help Sally hand out candy. I was working the 5:30 pm to 2 am shift in the ER, so I missed the neighborhood kids trick-or-treating in their round Harry Potter glasses and thunderbolt scars drawn on their foreheads, and the kids with pirate eyepatches and plastic sabers.

A few weeks later, Sally showed me pictures she had taken of Sarah, dressed up to hand out candy. Sarah posed with her face tilted down, eyes staring up boldly into the camera. Her face had a thin layer of white makeup. Her smile was in the shape of an angel's bow, black lipstick stark against the corpse-colored skin. A thin stream of scarlet trickled from the corner of her mouth. Blue-gray mascara was smeared across each eyelid and shanks of jet-black hair swept through her blond bangs.

She stood with her hips at a tilt: right knee jutting forward, the red sheen of crushed velvet stretching tightly across hips and breasts. A press-on tattoo of a panther was climbing her forearm, the claws leaving red dots on her skin. Her plastic press-on fingernails were tipped in red. The nails were sharp and pointed. A spider sat motionless on the bare skin just above the hint of cleavage. She had crowned herself with a plastic tiara. At the center of the crown was a crystal butterfly with wings of blue sapphires and swirls of red rhinestones.

No pastel pinks or baby blues, no gossamer wings or Tinker Bell wands. It was all blood and sex and black widow spiders. My daughter had stretched the canvas of her imagined self, and had chosen a darker palate.

The inevitability of Sarah reaching puberty, and the possibility of her getting pregnant, had bubbled disturbingly in the back of my mind for years. People often refer to children with Down syndrome as being "so affectionate." Sometimes it seemed that the ability to love another person had become one of the stigmata of the condition. But Sarah was more reserved than many of her peers. She'd laugh without restraint, and would give you an enthusiastic hug if she knew and liked you. But if you were a stranger, she'd pull away. I was glad of that.

Sally and I had spoken with other parents about birth control. One time, at Special Olympics, another mom and I were talking.

"I don't get it," she said. "We can sign the forms to get her tonsils taken out, or her appendix, but not to get her tubes tied." She continued to stare at her daughter. "The doctor said we couldn't sign for reproductive surgery, but we could get around it with a hysterectomy. We'd just have to say that she couldn't maintain her personal hygiene when she had a period. But a hysterectomy seems drastic."

———

It did seem drastic, and it didn't make sense—until I learned the history of forced sterilization programs in the United States. In my home state, North Carolina, between 1929 and 1974, 7,600 "feeble-minded" people were sterilized against their will.

The laws forcing people to submit to sterilization were the result of the eugenics movement. "Positive eugenics" involved encouraging people with desirable traits—high moral standing, intelligence, a strong work ethic—to have more babies. "Negative eugenics" involved keeping the undesirables from reproducing. There was an assumption and fear that underpinned the field of eugenics: that lazy, dimwitted people reproduced more quickly than the virtuous, hardworking ones. Society would soon be overrun by sloth, drunkenness, and poverty, to the peril of all.

The eugenics movement began in Victorian England, and soon became powerful in the United States. Eugenicists successfully lobbied for anti-immigration laws to keep America white, and for laws to prevent interracial marriage. To be clear, eugenicists weren't big-bellied blue-collar guys muttering about the wops who won't work and the darkies who do it like rabbits in the bushes. No; eugenicists were educated. They were forward-thinking intellectuals. Progressives. Harvard, Columbia, and Cornell—they all offered courses in eugenics.

In 1920, Margaret Sanger, a proponent of women's rights, sexual education, and birth control, wrote the following: "The lower down in the scale of human development we go the less sexual control we find. It is said that the aboriginal Australian, the lowest known species of the human family, just a step higher than the chimpanzee in brain development, has so little sexual control that police authority alone prevents him from obtaining sexual satisfaction on the streets." Said more plainly, she thought that, were it not for the police, the natives would be fucking in the streets.

In 1921, Sanger founded the American Birth Control League, a forerunner of Planned Parenthood. She supported eugenic sterilization (forcing the feeble-minded to submit to sterilization), but she opposed killing subnormal children. The subnormal adults, she wrote, could be segregated or sterilized.

Thirty states passed laws allowing doctors to perform sterilization operations on feeble-minded people against their will and against the will of their family. In 1924, the Virginia State Colony for Epileptics and Feebleminded chose a seventeen-year-old named Carrie Buck as their first case. Carrie had been committed to the Virginia Colony after delivering a child out of wedlock—proof of her promiscuity.

Carrie's biological mother had, in earlier times, been committed to the Virginia Colony for immorality, prostitution, and for having syphilis. The doctors at the Virginia Colony thought that any child that Carrie conceived would inherit the same feeble-mindedness and sluttiness that she had inherited from her mother.

Carrie fought her case all the way up to the US Supreme Court, where Justice Oliver Wendell Holmes, Jr., wrote, "Three generations of imbeciles are enough."

At 9:30 in the morning of October 19, 1927, Carrie was given a general anesthetic, and a doctor named J. H. Bell swabbed her belly with antiseptic, cut through her skin and the muscles of her abdominal wall, and stuck his gloved hands down into her belly. He groped around until he found a fallopian tube, delicate and pink, about five inches long. The tubes, also called oviducts, carry eggs from the ovaries to the uterus. Holding one of the tubes in his fingers, Dr. Bell cut out a one-inch chunk. He then put a suture around the stump, and tied a knot that he cinched down tighter and tighter, until the tube was crushed shut. Dr. Bell then swabbed the ends with carbolic acid, and gave them a second swipe with alcohol. He repeated the procedure on the other tube. He then sewed her belly closed, and applied a bandage.

Done.

In the United States, we sterilized people with intellectual disability until the 1970s. 70,000 Americans were sterilized without consent.

When Adolf Hitler wrote *Mein Kampf,* he was already a big fan of the US eugenics movement. He wrote, "I have studied with great interest the laws of several American states concerning prevention of reproduction by people whose progeny would, in all probability, be of no value or be injurious to the racial stock."

With the rise of the National Socialist Party in Germany, eugenics blossomed to its full potential. Using laws based on those in the United States, Germany outlawed interracial marriage, and began enforcing sterilization of people who were thought to be genetically inferior. Hitler took it one step further than Margaret Sanger would have and authorized a secret program to "euthanize" sub-par children, using starvation and lethal injection.[47] A book co-authored in 1920 by an attorney and a psychiatrist, *Die Freigabe der Vernichtung Lebensunwerten Lebens* (*Allowing the Destruction of Life Unworthy of Life*) provided the philosophical and ethical justification for killing disabled children.

This soon evolved into Action T4, a secret program to rid Germany of all people—children and adults—who could weaken the Aryan blood line: people with schizophrenia, epilepsy, congenital deafness, Huntington's chorea, and mental retardation—they planned to kill them all. The program's organizers used medical language in their documents—"euthanasia" and "final treatment"—as if killing a patient was just another medical therapy. No attempt was made to pass legislation to make it legal, as they had with compulsory sterilization. Instead, they kept it secret, using a letter from Hitler, on his official stationery, as authori-

zation. They started by injecting individual people. In the
Eglfing-Haar institution, outside Munich, the pediatric
ward had a special room exclusively for that purpose. A
nurse stocked the room and assisted the physician with the
procedure. She kept a potted geranium in the windowsill
of the sunlit room, to keep it bright and cheerful.[48] The
progam expanded, and after experimenting with the most
humane way to kill large groups at the same time, they settled on carbon monoxide.

When Hitler decided to rid Germany of Jews, gypsies,
and political opponents, the basic technologies and proce-
dures were ready.

In 2011, the North Carolina legislature made efforts toward
reparations to the individuals and families affected by forced
sterilization.[49] The state House of Representatives set aside
$10 million in the state budget, making North Carolina the
first state to try to make compensation to victims of eugenic
sterilization, but in June of 2012, the state Senate refused
to fund the program. Only after I learned about this did it
become clear to me why the genetics counselor, and our OB
doctor, had shied away from the subject of sterilization.

I never pushed the issue, and had hesitated even to bring

the subject up. There was something intrusive and unseemly about a father wanting to have his daughter sterilized.

Sally assumed that once Sarah was in a group home, staff members would make sure she took her prescribed birth control pills. It's not that we expected her to be sexually promiscuous, but we hoped she'd fall in love, have a boyfriend, maybe get married. But if we couldn't sign for a tubal ligation, we surely wouldn't be able to sign for an abortion. And if Sarah wasn't competent to sign for her own tubal ligation, how could she sign for her own abortion? If she got pregnant, who would raise her child after Sally and I died?

Chapter Eighteen

Walking past Sarah's bedroom, I noticed her sitting alone. She was nineteen. Her hands were folded in her lap, and her legs dangled off the edge of the bed. She wore black canvas Mary Jane shoes. No music was playing, and no books were spread out on the bed. No crayons were scattered around. She was staring at a chest of drawers with a beveled oval mirror in a matching mahogany frame.

"You okay?" I asked, pausing in the doorway.

She looked at me. "I guess so." She turned to look at the chest of drawers again.

As far as I knew, the morning had been good: I hadn't had to ask Sarah to turn down her music. I hadn't heard her yelling at Sally as she brushed the tangles out of her hair. No fussing about brushing her teeth.

"What is it?" I asked.

"I've got a question." She looked me in the face again.

"Okay." I stepped into the room. "Shoot." I loved answering questions—knowing stuff, and explaining things.

"When will I get over Down syndrome?"

I sat in the chair next to her bed. It was a rocking chair with curved oak slats.

Sarah's head was tilted to the side. Her tone sounded speculative. Maybe it was a rhetorical question—a conversational gambit. "When you'll get over Down syndrome?" I asked. I rocked slightly back and forward.

"Yeah," she said. She looked me in the eyes. "When?"

I sat still and gathered my thoughts. Her Down syndrome notwithstanding, Sarah was bright, and she read facial expressions well. She had a surprisingly good vocabulary. But her thinking was concrete. And she didn't like it when someone beat around the bush.

She waited.

"It's not something you get over," I finally said. "It's not like a cold, or a cough, or a heart attack." Sally and I had always thought it important not to be bashful about Down syndrome. It was a medical fact. No cause for shame or squeamishness. Once, when Sarah was ten, I asked her what she thought having Down syndrome meant. She said, "It means I have to try harder." I liked that definition: it was pragmatic, and it dodged the pitfalls of seeing Down syndrome as good or bad, as a blessing or a curse. It was something Sarah had—not who she was.

Making this distinction hadn't felt like fudging. Most of us would acknowledge that our bodies give form to who we are: male or female. Short or tall. Skinny or fat. Descended from Africans, Asians, or Europeans. But our genes don't make us who we are: we define ourselves by the decisions we make. And every day, each of us bumps up against our limitations. Same with Sarah.

I just didn't know how to articulate all of this in terms she'd grasp. Her strengths were in the specific and physical, not the abstract. And anything I said could sound glib and unearned. I had no idea what it was like to live in Sarah's skin. I'd never had to struggle so hard to do the things that come easily to others. And anyway, that wasn't her question.

Sarah stared at me. Didn't blink.

"You know how Mommy has curly hair, and you have straight hair?"

"Yeah."

"It's because of her genes," I said. "Not jeans, jeans." I pinched the denim of my pants leg, and gave it a tug. "Genes like in chromosomes." I paused. "The genes in Mommy's cells give her curly hair and gray eyes, and the genes in your cells give you blond hair and hazel eyes."

She stared at me.

"Genes also give you Down syndrome," I continued. Sarah knew the term trisomy 21, and that it involved chromosomes. Genes.

"Yeah, I know," she said. "But when will I get over it?" Her face was motionless.

Sometimes I wished that she were just a few degrees more intellectually disabled, or a few degrees less.

"Down syndrome isn't something that goes away." I waited. "It's something you'll have forever. Like blond, straight hair and hazel eyes."

She nodded slightly, as if to herself, and then looked down at her hands. "I'm tired of it." Her shoulders slumped. Her hair fell down on either side of her face.

"I know you are," I said. "Me too."

Her face remained hidden behind the curtains of her hair, and I didn't know what she was thinking. Or feeling. I wondered if saying "Me too" was a mistake. I wanted her to know that she wasn't alone and that her feelings were valid. Maybe I should have given her a pep talk instead. Tell her how Down syndrome was really not that bad—that she should think of herself as "alternatively enabled." Make my voice sound upbeat. But if I had, she would have looked at me and shook her head, wondering where I came up with such Suzy Sunshine horseshit.

I wanted so much for her to feel better. Not hurt. I got out of the chair and sat next to her on the edge of her bed. "Your mom and I love you." I put an arm around her shoulders. "We believe in you."

I felt false, like I was reciting lines in a play. But the fact is, we *did* love her and believe in her. I squeezed her shoulder. "You got that, right?" I leaned forward to make eye contact. "Straight hair or curly, gray eyes or hazel, we love you. We're proud of you." I paused. "Whether you have Down syndrome or not."

She shrugged her right shoulder, and twisted her body away from me.

I took my hand from her shoulder.

"You can go now." She didn't look up. I didn't know if she was reassuring me that she was okay, or dismissing me.

"Do you want me to go?"

"Yes," she said. "Please."

If I was a better dad, I might have said, "You're perfect the way you are." Isn't that what each of us longs to hear? But after all of the Early Intervention, the sign language, the walker, the occupational therapists, physical therapists, speech therapists—the small army of people who had helped Sally and me prepare Sarah for as broad a future as possible—the words would have sounded false. At least to me. Probably to her, as well. But each and every one of us has something about ourselves we'd like to change. We may be quick to anger. Unmotivated. Lazy. Too ambitious. Our asses may sag and our bellies may have stretch marks. No such thing as an unflawed human.

"Please," she repeated, stressing the word.

I stood and walked to the door. I wanted to tell her I

admired her courage. But she had asked me, twice, to leave. I paused at the door. "I think you're great," I said. "Just like you are." There. I finally found the right words. The pressure that had been building in my chest began to dissipate.

"Please, Dad," my daughter told me. "Just go."

Chapter Nineteen

When Sarah was twenty-two, I drove her to Atlanta to visit Aunt Susan, Sally's younger sister. Susan had flair and an eye for fashion, and would help Sarah pick out a new wardrobe. Sally trusted her to help Sarah avoid combining stripes, paisleys, and polka dots when she dressed.

I would get some father–daughter time on the six-and-a-half-hour drive. We were in my new car, a Chrysler 300. Black, with chrome wheels and pearl-gray leather seats and a walnut steering wheel, it was the first luxury car I'd ever owned.

Sarah's pink nylon backpack sat on the floor beside her feet. She reached down, her movements slow and deliberate, as she hoisted it into her lap. She let out a deep breath. She told me that she'd brought me something, but she talked too fast and her words ran together in a thick-tongued slur—the way they had all her life.

"Say it again." My response was automatic. I set my face in a smile. "Speak slowly, and say each word carefully." When Sarah was in elementary school, a speech therapist showed Sally and me how to pat the fingers of our right hand against the palm of our left—one pat at the beginning of each and every word, to make each word stand out. We would have Sarah do the same thing, particularly when she was tired or excited, and words began to run together. But she was now too old for techniques from elementary school.

She tried again, frowning. "I *said,*" then the words slurred again and I couldn't understand them. She stopped and looked at me. "At work," she continued. "To drink on the way." For the past couple of years, Sarah had been going to a sheltered workshop—a nonprofit organization that arranged piecework for people with intellectual disability: putting together promotional packets for Burt's Bees, or sorting nuts, bolts, and washers. She didn't like it. "I get bored."

Sarah's goal had been to get a job in the community. She had recently started a job bagging groceries at Harris Teeter for four hours a day, three days a week. A job coach from the sheltered workshop went with her.

Sarah unzipped her pack and pulled out a bottled Frappuccino. "It's Starbucks," she said, handing it to me.

The Frappuccino cap made a little inward sigh as the vacuum released.

"I got it because I knew you like it," Sarah said.

"Delicious," I said, holding it up and glancing from the interstate, to the label, and back to the road again.

Sarah let out another pent-up breath, and reached into

her backpack again. "I brought a Diet Coke for me." Clasping the plastic bottle between her legs, she unscrewed the cap. "Don't worry. I won't spill it."

Sarah sipped. I sipped.

The tires hummed.

She looked over to me. "I also brought *Mamma Mia!* I think you'll like it. It's rock and roll."

Actually, it's ABBA.

Sarah slid the disc into the dashboard, looked over at me, and turned the volume up. She paused, glanced at me, and turned it up again.

We drove in silence, listening to the music.

The song ended and Sarah pressed the eject button. "Did I tell you about my new screenplay?"

"I don't think you have," I said.

"It's called *Almost Royal*, or maybe, *Royal or Not*."

I nodded. Another screenplay. Sarah had written scores of them. The title page had a crayon drawing of four tall, thin people, hands bulging with five sausage-like fingers, faces with three tiny circles for the eyes and nose, and a simple upturned curve of a mouth. The second page always had a list of actors she planned to use, and the third page consisted of a couple of paragraphs describing the plot. Then it was four or five blank pages, stapled together in the upper left corner.

"It's about a girl who is switched at birth, and her real

mother is the queen of a small little country like Ireland, but not Ireland." Her enunciation was good. "No one realizes she's a princess, because her parents are American—not her real parents—the ones who think they're the real parents." She took a sip of Diet Coke.

I nodded along with the cadence of her speech. "Sounds good. Thanks for speaking slowly and clearly."

"I am." She waited a moment. "The princess has special needs, so when they find out she's a princess, it makes it a little complicated."

"Special needs?" I glanced over at her.

"Down syndrome."

I nodded again.

"She's in high school, in a special needs class, but she takes some classes with the other kids." Sarah looked over at me. "You know, like art."

"Sure," I said. Sarah had taken art with the regular kids. They had previously called it "mainstreaming," but they then started calling it "inclusion." I'd never been clear as to what the difference was.

"And she has a boyfriend, who doesn't have special needs, but her parents don't like him because he's African American."

"Okay."

"Her parents aren't racist. They think he's using her."

"Using her?" I kept my voice neutral. *Is some normal kid fucking my daughter?*

"To be with the popular kids."

"Do they know she's a princess?"

"Not yet." Sarah took another sip of Diet Coke. "But when Julie Andrews discovers that her real daughter is an American with Down syndrome, she has to decide which is more important: truth or fiction."

"*Truth or Fiction,*" I said. "That might make a good title."

"Not really." She looked out the window, then back at me. "*Royal or Not.* It sounds better." We rode along, and the wind and tires made their soothing highway sounds.

Sarah turned in her seat and carefully put her Diet Coke in the cupholder of the console between us. "Like, what if Charlie in *Willy Wonka* had Down syndrome?" Sarah let the question hang.

"Okay." I kept my eyes on the car ahead of us.

"It's basically the Cinderella story. Only, not the Disney Cinderella. To really understand the whole thing, you've got to go back to the Cinderella story before Disney did it." She settled back in her seat, and began warming up to the subject. Sarah loved the Cinderella story. Unrecognized beauty.

"Has some kid in your inclusion class been touching you?"

"What?" Her head swiveled on her neck.

"Has some kid been touching you?"

"*Dad.* This is fiction." She spread her hands, palms up. "It didn't really happen. I made it up."

"Sometimes fiction is based on a true story," I said, glancing over at her.

"Not this time," she said. "Anyway, I already have a boyfriend. He's forty-two."

I'll kill the bastard.

"At least he wants to be my boyfriend," Sarah said. "I told him he's too old."

"Where did you meet him?"

"Special Olympics. He runs track."

"He has special needs?"

"Yeah." She caught her lower lip between her teeth as she put the CD in its case. She snapped it shut. "Kyle, in my OCS class likes me too, but I need someone more in touch with their emotions." OCS stood for "occupational course of study," which was one click up from special education.

"How old is he?"

"My age." Sarah shrugged. "I guess."

"Is he cute?"

"Yeah, but he has autism." She pulled another CD from her bag. "He doesn't listen very well."

"So, what happens to the princess that was switched at birth?"

"Her boyfriend breaks up with her right before Julie Andrews announces that she's a princess."

"Who would play the boyfriend?"

"I don't know. Someone like Eddie Murphy, I guess."

"Does he feel bad once he finds out that the girl's a princess?"

"Oh, yeah," Sarah said. "Big time."

"Does Julie Andrews have a husband?"

"They're divorced. So the movie's a little like *The Parent Trap*. The princess tries to get them back together."

"Who plays the dad?"

"Johnny Depp."

"Sounds good."

I held my Frappuccino toward Sarah, and she clinked her Diet Coke against it.

She slid another CD into the dash. *The Lion King*. Sarah and I settled into the opening Zulu chorus of "The Circle of Life," the harmonies plaintive and mysterious.

The next day, I dropped off Aunt Susan and Sarah at Old Navy and went to a Starbucks in the same mall. A couple of hours later, they had filled a cart and gave me a call to meet them in the checkout line.

I saw them before they saw me. Aunt Susan hooked a strand of hair behind her ear, and leaned over to listen to Sarah. Sarah gestured with her hand and bobbed her head the way she does when she's been asked to repeat herself. Aunt Susan nodded and straightened up. Sarah said something else and Aunt Susan patted her shoulder, rubbed it gently, and patted it again.

When I walked up, Aunt Susan said, "She wanted some striped leotards. They were cute, but she doesn't have anything they'd go with."

Sarah looked up at Aunt Susan's face, smiled, and scrunched her shoulders. If it had been her mother, or me, she would have voiced an objection.

I glanced into the cart. There was a puffy white jacket, fake fur trimming the hood. Several knit shirts in solid colors. A khaki skirt. Black pants. It would be hard to mismatch anything in the cart.

———

Sarah and I spent the weekend with Aunt Susan and Uncle William. Sarah and her cousins—one eight years old, and one six—watched Disney movies in the playroom of the finished basement, while Susan, William, and I talked upstairs. Books. Movies. Favorite recipes.

On the drive home, Sarah asked, "What would happen if you and mom got divorced?" She loved the movie *The Parent Trap*—both the 1961 version and the remake in 1998. It was about identical twins, separated as babies when their parents divorced. The twins later meet at a summer camp and conspire to get their parents back together. After *Cinderella*, it was Sarah's favorite plotline.

"We'll never get divorced." I looked over at her, and then back to the eighteen-wheeler in front of us.

"I know," she said. "But I'm just asking. What if."

"But we won't."

"Would I move in with Aunt Susan?"

"Would you like to?" I took my foot off the accelerator to get some more room between me and the truck.

Sarah nodded and shrugged, as if it went without saying. "How come?"

"She's younger." Her voice had a teasing lilt. "And she's cooler."

I nodded and shrugged. It went without saying. "Sorry, kiddo, but we'll never get divorced."

Her shoulders sagged.

"Till death do us part," I said, placing the back of my wrist against my forehead and spreading my fingers as I tilted my head back.

"Oh, Dad," Sarah said, "You're always so dramatic."

Sarah shook her head, and pulled her ABBA CD from her backpack.

———

When we got home, Sarah showed Sally her new clothes. "The credit card caught on fire," Sarah said, laughing loudly.

"What?" Sally looked over at me.

"Aunt Susan and Sarah spent so much the credit card smoked when I ran it through the slot."

"Ohhh," Sally said. "Well I'm glad you got your clothes before a fire started."

The next day I was sitting in my chair in the living room, reading, and Sarah walked up. "You and mom getting along okay?"

"I think so," I said. "Why? She seem mad or something?" I looked up from my paperback.

"No." Sarah shook her head.

I waited, but she didn't say anything else. I went back to *Tishomingo Blues*.

Sarah stood, looking at me.

"But if you *did* get divorced," she said, "would I move in with Aunt Susan?"

"Absolutely," I said, closing my paperback. "In fact, we can probably send you down to Atlanta right now. Next bus."

"You're kidding, aren't you?"

"Put your new clothes in a paper sack, pin Aunt Susan's name and address on your shirt, and put you on a Greyhound."

"You're joking." She shook her head. "You guys will never get divorced." She turned to go, then stopped. "But if you do, it'll be goodbye Durham and hello Hot Atlanta."

Chapter Twenty

We had put Sarah's name on a waiting list for a group home when she was still in grade school. We thought of doing this because of a movie we'd seen at the UNC student union, years before Sarah was born—before we even got married. Sally and I tended toward inexpensive dates: walks along the banks of the Eno River, browsing in bookstores, and free movies at the student union. One documentary we saw was *Best Boy*: it was about a fifty-two-year-old man with mental retardation. Philly still lived with his parents, who were in their seventies. The movie was about the pain and difficulty of preparing Philly for the time his parents would be too old and infirm to take care of him.

The movie stayed with me. When Sarah was nine, I called Residential Services Incorporated, a nonprofit organization in Chapel Hill started by parents of special needs children and UNC faculty. Cradling the receiver, I explained that it would be years before Sarah would be going to a group home, but that my wife and I wanted to know what the options were, to plan ahead.

The person on the phone arranged for Sally and me to visit a group home, as if it were the most routine thing in the world.

A few weeks later, we stood in front of a house in an upper-middle-class neighborhood of old trees and well-tended yards. From the outside, it looked like any other house on the block, except for the large red pipe jutting out of the wall next to the front door, for the building's sprinkler system.

Loblolly pines shaded the lot from the midafternoon sun, and a thick layer of needles softened our steps. Inside, the furniture didn't exactly match, but the rooms felt homey, and lived in. The kitchen was spacious, and had an oval table with lots of chairs around it. One of the residents was there, alone. Our guide introduced us.

I wondered if it was safe for a resident to be there without a staff member. I didn't ask. The young man was eager to tell us. He had regular features and carefully brushed hair, but he smiled too quickly, and looked too intently in our faces as he spoke.

"I can stay here." He nodded. "By myself." He pointed to the phone. "I only call for emergencies. It is not a toy. I keep the doors locked. I stay inside." He pointed to the clock. "At three o'clock the van comes back from OE and we all take a walk and then we watch TV."

Sally and I nodded along as he spoke.

"Teresa is my girlfriend." His face was smoothly shaved, except for one small patch of dark stubble on his chin. He smiled broadly. "She lives at Jones Ferry Road."

"One of the other group homes," our guide told us.

I inwardly winced at the term "group home" said out loud in front of a resident.

He nodded, to confirm what our guide had told us.

"How often do you see her?" I asked.

"Fun Fridays." He shrugged. "Picnics. Times like that."

"A church in Durham sponsors Fun Friday. Pizza and activities once a month." Our guide turned to the resi-dent. "You also see Teresa on movie night and at Special Olympics."

He nodded again.

I was glad the young man seemed happy. Maybe Sarah would be too.

———

When John and Sam moved away, it would be to college, or the military, or a job. For Sarah, it would be a group home. One evening, when Sarah was a preteen, she invited us to watch her favorite TV show, *Sabrina, the Teenage Witch.* Sarah sprawled on her belly on the floor, cradling her chin in her hands. I sat in a chair, and Sally sat on the couch.

As the show began, it became clear that the spunky young woman with blond hair and large breasts was Sabrina. She lived with two aunts, who were also witches, as best as I could tell. I glanced over at Sally.

"Is Sabrina supposed to be a high school kid?" She looked more like a cocktail waitress than a high school kid. Or a witch.

"Dad," Sarah said, stretching out the word. She twisted her body to look at me. "She's already finished high school. Now she lives in a group home. Duh!!!!"

If she left right after high school, she would leave before her younger brothers, which is how most regular people in a family do it. Note the choice of word—"regular," instead of "normal." Sally and I struggled for years to find the right phrase. If we used the word "normal" to describe non-Down syndrome people, it would imply that Sarah was "abnormal." Didn't seem quite fair, or accurate. She wasn't abnormal. She had Down syndrome. "Regular kid" seemed a less pejorative converse to Sarah's situation. But no matter how carefully we phrased it, once we used the term "regular kid," or "special needs," or "intellectually disabled," we created a divide. It was just another way of saying "us" and "them."

Sarah was on a waiting list for a good group home, which
seemed to be her best option. But even a good group home
seemed second-best: I had a half-formed fear that the relationships Sarah would have—the conversations, love, affec-
tion, respect, anger, problems—would be "less than" those
in a regular family.

But just as a wheelchair can afford mobility, a good group
home can provide community, security, and independence.
And with the improvement of medical care for people with
Down syndrome, it was possible that Sarah would outlive
Sally and me. Then what? Sally and I didn't want to use her
brothers as her backup plan: they'd have their own lives.
Sarah's life deserved its own trajectory, independent of my
health or Sally's, and independent of her brothers.

I once heard a radio interview in which a man with para-
plegia responded to a question about being confined to his
wheelchair: He said his wheelchair was the exact opposite of
confining: it's what gave him mobility.

Once he had pointed it out, it seemed obvious; but as a
non-disabled person, I would never have seen it that way.
Just like the interviewer, my point of view as an able-bodied
person had led me to make unfounded assumptions.

Perhaps my vocabulary, as much as my experience, had limited my understanding. The terms "disabled" and "able" are as binary as a light switch. But the reality is that both conditions exist on a spectrum. And all of us, with the exception of those who die instantly in car crashes or cardiac arrests, will experience some disability before we die.

Our bodies age. Put on weight. We get fitted for bifocals. Trifocals. Make little "oomph" sounds getting out of chairs. No matter how many miles we run or how many yoga poses we twist ourselves into, and no matter how many quarts of pomegranate juice we consume, our bodies will eventually wear out. Our arteries become inelastic. Our telomeres fray. People with disabilities confront their human frailties sooner than the rest of us, even though we share a common destiny: through accident or wear-and-tear, our bodies ultimately betray us.

My assumptions about disability were so ingrained, and unconscious, that until my daughter was born with Down syndrome, I didn't really even *see* disabled people. I just saw wheelchairs and crutches and canes.

From the moment that Sarah was born, Sally—a stay-at-home mother—had borne most of the care of Sarah's special needs: scheduling Individual Education Plans, keeping doctor's appointments, listening to her stories, reminding her to speak clearly.

When Sarah was in her senior year of high school, a spot came open in a group home in Durham. Sally jumped on it. Sarah could finish out her senior year from the group home. She was nineteen.

On the day Sarah moved, the dogwood tree in our side yard blossomed white against an April sky. On the front porch, Sarah's new entertainment center glowed pink with a fresh coat of paint. Sally had bought it three weeks previously at the unfinished furniture store. John sanded every surface and brushed on the white primer, and Sally applied two coats of pink latex paint. The intensity of the color surprised us; on the paint chip the color was as light and airy as cotton candy, but once Sally had brushed on a quart of the color, it darkened.

We planned to move Sarah's possessions on Saturday. Sarah would spend one more night in our house, and then move into her new home on Sunday.

When I asked Sarah if she would be glad to get to her new home, she had said, "Sort of." It was one of her shorthand ways of acknowledging conflicting thoughts and emotions she couldn't quite articulate.

"Sort of?" I asked, reflecting back, hoping that she would say more. She raised her right shoulder half an inch as if to say, *Yeah, that just about sums it up.*

————

"Big," Sam said. He stared at the tall, wide piece of furniture glowing on our front porch. "Pink, too." He was thirteen.

Sarah walked past, carrying a paper sack of clothing to the van. She paused at the front step. Even though she was nineteen, she was small and looked young, and waitresses routinely gave her a child's menu and put a few crayons in front of her. "I'm not a child," Sarah would say, her inflection neutral, informative. Sarah's words were torqued in a way that seemed typical of people with Down syndrome. There was a slight slur, and a lilt: the sound was more child-like than slow-witted.

"Can I have an adult menu, please?" she'd say. Our family understood her because we knew her voice, and had heard the same conversation over and over. If the server understood her, she'd say, "Of course," and scoop up the crayons and kid's menu. But as often as not, the waitress would glance at Sally or me. "Sarah is nineteen," one of us would say. "She'd prefer an adult menu."

The waitress usually blushed, scooped up the crayons and child's menu, and hurried away. John and Sam put their heads down, staring at their laminated menus.

———

"You're going to have a VCR and cable TV," Sam said to Sarah. "In your room."

She stood at the top step, her back to us.

"It'll be great," Sam said, "having a TV right there in your own room." Our family had one television, closed up in a cabinet in the living room. We didn't have cable.

"I know," Sarah said, without turning to face Sam. She watched her feet as she stepped down the three brick stairs from the porch to the walk. Her hair hung down either side, shielding her face.

Sam looked at me.

I took a slow deep breath. When I exhaled, my chest still felt empty.

We both watched Sarah walk toward the van.

I ducked my head back into the cabinet. It was made of pine and pressboard, with a thin plywood back, intended to be used as a hutch. It had no holes in the back for the wires to go through. I pulled my head out. "I'm going to use a hole saw, with the inch-and-a-half blade, make two holes, and then connect them." I gestured toward the plywood at the back of the cabinet. "For the wires."

Sam glanced at the tools spread out on the floor of the porch.

"It's hard to tell what she's thinking, or feeling," I said to Sam.

"No kidding."

"Hard to tell what I'm feeling too," I said. I pointed to a tape measure just out of reach on the floor. "Hand me the tape measure?"

Sam stooped and picked it up. His blond hair was long-ish and fell down in front of his eyes.

Using the tape measure, square, and a pencil, I marked off a slot, an inch and a half high and six inches wide. I tightened the chuck around the bit in the center of the hole saw. It made a perfect hole. The drill was yellow plastic, but felt heavy and solid in my hand. The bit went through the plywood easily, throwing pink sawdust in the air, then a brief dusting of white from the primer coat, and then raw wood.

"Maybe I'm feeling a little guilty," I said to Sam.

No answer.

I pulled my head out of the cabinet, but Sam had gone back inside. If there had been an opportunity for me to help Sam navigate the emotions incurred by the departure of his older sister, I had hoped to let the moment unfold naturally—without me botching it by trying to explain it too much, or telling him what he should be feeling. I sat back on my butt.

———

"The cabinet is looking good."

Sally stood behind me, on the porch. Her hair, turning gray, was pulled back from her forehead. I was glad when she quit dyeing it. The strands of silver and white are so much more vibrant than the monochromatic brown that results from dye. And letting her hair turn gray showed a quiet courage, a defiance of society's expectations. I respected that. Of course, Sally was lucky—she had so much hair, wave after wave of curls, parted in the center. That day, she had just pulled the frothy, chaotic mass of hair from her face. She was fifty-two. We'd been married twenty-two years.

Sally stood straight, chin up, shoulders back, feet slightly splayed: muscle memory of ballet lessons as a child and modern dance lessons as an adult. She had a small frame and wide shoulders.

"It'll be another fifteen, twenty minutes," I said, pointing to the pink hutch.

"No rush."

Sally hummed quietly, almost audibly. That's how I knew she was feeling stressed. When I saw her lips curl up and her head tilt just half a degree, and she did this little nod of hers, I knew she was faking. "You probably know about 25 percent of what I think and feel," she told me once, at our marriage counselor's. I was surprised her estimate was that high.

"I've got about another hour or so of packing," Sally said. "Odds and ends." She touched my shoulder and turned to go inside.

John sauntered onto the porch. He was fifteen. His blond hair was pillow-flattened on the left, and stuck up on the right. He took a bite of a frosted blueberry Pop-Tart and examined the purple jam oozing from the edge of the pastry.

I glanced at my watch. Eleven thirty. "Up early," I said.

"It's Saturday." He rolled his napkin into a tight ball and tossed it over his shoulder. It landed on the top shelf of the entertainment center. "Three points." He made a fist, held it in front of his mouth, and belched silently.

I reached up, picked up his napkin, and tossed it to him. "Give me a hand loading this in about half an hour?"

"Sure." He strolled back inside, tossing the napkin up and down in the palm of his hand.

"Mom said I could swing." Sarah clomped out through the front door, to the swing that hung from chains at the end of the porch. She took a small step backward, and then another, until the backs of her legs bumped the front of the swing: it was four feet wide, made of oak slats, and painted white. She gripped the swing with both hands and sat down. She moved slowly and deliberately, shifting her weight until the backs of her knees were against the front of the swing. She then pulled a pair of headphones over her ears and opened the top of her fanny pack. She fiddled with the buttons. I could faintly hear the tinny sound of a Broadway show tune leaking out from around the edges of her headphones.

"Turn it down," I said, loudly. "Turn it down." Sarah had a mild congenital hearing loss, and loud music would only worsen it. But I also wanted her to turn the volume down because when it was loud, she couldn't hear herself sing. She yelled and shrieked. Neighbors commented on it, always couched in a way to let us know that they understood that Sarah had Down syndrome and the sound of her singing didn't bother them, per se, but it penetrated through their walls and into their living rooms.

In the swing, Sarah went as high as she could, pumping her legs purposefully. At the zenith of each swooshing moment, the swing's chains were almost horizontal. It looked as if she could almost touch the ceiling of the porch with the toe of her Mary Janes. Then she swooped backward until she was looking down onto the red leaves of the Nandina bush at the five-foot drop-off at the end of the porch. At the last minute, when it looked as if she would tumble into the bush and then bounce to the ground, she hurtled forward again, centrifugal force keeping her in the swing.

Sally and I had given up on asking her to swing less vigorously. "She's burning off energy," Sally said. "Let's leave her alone."

"Do I need to take your CD player away?" I dusted the sawdust from the entertainment center from my palms.

Sarah scowled, turned the music down, and closed the flap to her CD player pouch. She settled back into the swing, and began pumping her legs to build up speed.

Having completed two holes in the back of the TV center, I drew a line from the top of one to the top of the other, and then a line from bottom to bottom. I plugged in the saber saw, and guided the toothy blur of the blade along each line, making a smooth cut, with only a fine fuzz of splinters on the upper edge. I sanded these down.

"Done," I said to Sarah in a loud voice.

She continued singing under her breath. We both knew

that as soon as I left the porch, she would crank up the volume. She probably wished I would hurry up.

"Now you can plug in your TV," I said, pointing to the
slot in the back of the entertainment center.

"I know."

I went inside. Sally was upstairs in Sarah's room, pulling
clothes from the closet and laying them on one of the twin
beds. The hangers made a clacking sound. The mattress,
bare of sheets and blankets, had a diamond-shaped pattern
stitched into the satiny blue fabric. Sarah's clothes tended
toward pastels that would coordinate easily.

Standing behind Sally, I put my hands on either side of
her waist, just above the belt line. "Lots to do," she said,
turning.

I put my forehead against her head. Her body felt tense
under my palms. "What?" I asked.

"Nothing." Sally pulled back. "I should have had all
this packed before today." When she was working as a
nurse-educator, Sally taught classes in assertiveness training
and time management, but she still struggled to get things
done on time.

"We'll get it all done," I said. "Can I help?"

"It would be easier if I did this part by myself. Keep it
organized."

"Okay."

She glanced at the chest of drawers. "That needs to go," she said. "Maybe take the drawers down first."

The drawers were surprisingly light, still filled with Sarah's socks and underwear. Her socks were small, with lace around the top, folded over, just so. Her underwear, sensibly cut, with picot trim and bow, came from the "big kid" page of a catalogue, several pages away from the lingerie other nineteen-year-olds might wear.

I ran my fingers across the drawer front. It was a fine piece of furniture, and had been her mother's when she was a child. It was mahogany, and the top edge was carved with flowers and leaves that curled and rolled into waves and ribbons. The kind of furniture that families pass down generation after generation. The soft, old patina would soon sit side by side with the raw pink of Sarah's new entertainment center. Neither Sally nor I mentioned that Sarah would never have a daughter to pass it on to.

John, Sam, and I loaded the truck with the pink entertainment center and the antique chest of drawers with matching bed frame. Sarah and Sally took her VCR tapes, clothes, and ribbons from Special Olympics out to the van.

I focused on the details of the move—not letting things

get dinged or dropped—so I wouldn't have to face the half-formed fear that we were not helping Sarah move onto the next stage of her life, so much as moving her out of ours.

The van was packed. The pickup truck loaded.

Sally eased the van away from the curb, Sarah in the front passenger seat, Sam in the back. John and I slowly followed in the truck. A mimosa tree with pink puffs of flowers was planted in the strip between the sidewalk and gutter, and the limbs of massive old oak trees arched up over the street. The tips of their branches intertwined at the center, forming a cool green umbrella of shade.

———

"I think she'll like this group home," I said, glancing through the rear window at the pink entertainment center towering up from the bed of the truck.

"She'll have a TV," John said, as he rolled down his window. "In her room."

We drove past the School of Science and Math, a public, live-in high school for gifted students. Thick old trees shaded expansive green lawns. We coasted to a stop behind the van at the traffic light on Broad Avenue: an auto parts store on our right, an oriental carpet store across the street. Sally looked into the rearview mirror and waved. Sarah turned in her seat to wave at us too. John and I waved back.

When the light turned green, we slowly pulled away from the intersection, moving into a different neighborhood. We passed three identical mill houses, varying only in color: pastel pink, green, and blue. Wooden screen doors sagged with rusted screens. We slowly cruised past an abandoned public school, flat roof, busted windows, ten-foot-high chain-link fence. An elderly woman with a cane in one hand and a shopping bag in the other stood at a bus stop. She leaned forward and stared down the street.

"I wonder what the other people will be like," John said.

I turned to look at him.

"You know, living in Sarah's group home."

"Probably some have Down syndrome, some with other disabilities." I hoped there would be someone Sarah's age.

We passed a house with sagging gutters, cars parked in the rutted mud of the yard. Grass grew high and shaggy in the yards. A dog, all teeth and bristling neck hair, lunged against a short chain.

I didn't think that anyone would put a group home in a neighborhood like this. If for no other reason, the employees wouldn't like it. But upper-class neighborhoods would be able to mount resistance to any plans to establish a group home.

We crossed Roxboro Road, where West Club Boulevard became East Club. At the corner, a taqueria, a tienda, and a carniceria were lined up right next to each other. One long banner of green, white, and red spanned the three storefronts. A phone booth leaned sideways; its door had been torn off and bare wires sprouted from the bracket on which a pay phone once hung.

We drove past more houses with bare front yards and too many cars. We drove past open spaces with scrub pines, weeds shaggy at the road's edge, woods farther back, oaks and maples, a spray of white flowers from a dogwood tree. Prefab metal buildings were surrounded by expansive asphalt parking lots, which in turn were surrounded by chain-link fences topped with three strands of razor wire.

We crossed a narrow, unnamed river. Snarls of trees and shrubs lined the banks, the high-water line marked by tatters of plastic bags, six-pack rings, and muddy bits of fabric too stiff to flutter in the breeze. Farther on, we passed the city dump, and the dropoff point for hazardous household waste.

"Glad it's sunny," I said.

"Really." He held a lacrosse stick between his legs, the butt on the floor of the cab, the basket up. He liked to carry it to practice cradling the ball. Sally and I wanted the move to be as positive as possible, so we encouraged John to bring his lacrosse stick, and Sam to bring his skateboard.

We drove past an abandoned outdoor movie theater, and then past an entrance to a new development of two-story houses.

Sally turned left onto the street and I followed. The first yard had carefully trimmed hedges and a freshly mowed lawn. In the second yard sat a red Firebird with a gray tarp thrown over the front of the car. Water had pooled and was pulling the tarp down into the engine compartment—the hood and engine were gone. Beside it, another red Firebird sat on flat tires, the driver's door crumpled in. It was a toss-up as to which car would be cannibalized to fix the other. A kid's trampoline sagged in the side yard, the fabric ripped and hanging down to the weeds below. On the house next door, rust spots, from nailheads that hadn't been caulked, bled into white painted siding. In the yard, a charcoal grill lay on its side, the bottom lacy with rust.

Sally pulled the van into the cul-de-sac at the end of the street. I pulled in behind her and looked at Sarah's future home. It was a low, featureless brick ranch house, newer than the other houses in the neighborhood. The front yard was an uninterrupted sweep of grass, and the bushes in front were trimmed to geometric precision, plumb and level. The house was built of tan brick and the windows were dark, the blinds closed.

The front door opened before we knocked. A woman with Down syndrome welcomed us. She took my hand as she talked. I couldn't understand what she was saying, and wondered if Sarah sounded that way to other people.

I glanced around the dark living room. A television in the corner was on, and offered the only light. Five middle-aged women slumped in overstuffed chairs. One of them was knitting. She looked up at us, and then back to her needles. The others didn't turn their faces from the TV. I tried to pull my hand free of the damp grip of the girl who had opened the door, but she didn't let go.

The regional coordinator was there. After welcoming us all, she directed her comments to Sarah. This was reassuring to me. Her manner was pleasantly official. The group home manager stood behind her—silent, large, and slow-moving.

The girl dropped my hand, and took Sarah's. She said something about "room." Sarah stepped back and wrung her hand free.

"Patty," the director said, "Sarah and her mother already know where her room is."

"Great," I said, smiling at Patty. "Sarah," I said, looking over at my daughter. "Can you show us your room?"

"Sure." Sarah's voice was low. I couldn't tell if she was embarrassed by the grown-ups staring at her, or if she was feeling nervous about meeting a group of people who knew each other already: like the first day of school for the new kid. She glanced up at Sally, who gestured down the hall with a tilt of her head.

Sarah led us, single file, down a short, dark hallway, and then turned left into another short hallway. I didn't know if the hall was dark because they were conserving electricity for environmental reasons, or if they were too cheap to keep the place well lit. This group home didn't seem as nice as the one we had visited in Chapel Hill. I wished that Residential Services had an opening.

Sarah's room was the last one on the right. It smelled of fresh paint and new carpet. I wondered what had happened to the woman who used to live there.

Sarah stood in the middle of the room with her hands at her sides. She turned to look at us.

"TV center here?" I pointed to the cable connection coming out of the wall.

Sarah nodded.

I glanced over to Sally, who gave a confirming wink.

Patty stood in the middle of the doorway. Her shoulders were rounded, like Sarah's. John and Sam stood behind her, looking into the room.

"Okay, then." I slipped past Patty. The boys followed me down the dark hallways, to the dim living room, and then outside. We blinked at the sunlight. I heard John and Sam both take deep breaths, and let them out. "We'll dolly in the pink thing," I said, "and carry in the rest."

Patty edged along the wall of the hallway as Sarah's possessions were brought into the room. Sally told us where to set up the bed, and where to put the chest of drawers and entertainment center. When we were finished, Sam and John went outside to skateboard down the driveway and onto the asphalt cul-de-sac. Sarah, Sally, and I stood in the small room and looked around.

"I'm spending the night at home?" Sarah asked. "With you all?" We had planned to move all of her things on Saturday, and for her to spend one more night in our house. The next day, she and Sally would go back and get her settled in.

"Yup," I said. "One last night."

Sarah nodded.

The three of us filed out to the living room. Sally and I smiled and waved to the regional manager, the group home manager, and Patty. The other ladies didn't look up from the television.

Outside, Sarah walked to the van and waited for Sally to unlock it with the clicker. She climbed in and shut the door.

Back at home, Sarah swung high, and sang loudly.

PART THREE

Chapter Twenty-One

"Residential Services called," Sally said, a few months after Sarah had moved out. "They're opening a new group home for young adults. They want to meet Sarah, to see if she'd be a good fit."

"You mean she has to interview?" I asked. We were sitting at the kitchen table after supper. John and Sam had taken off with friends. The house Sarah was living in was dark and small, and I felt that we'd failed to deliver on the good group home we'd been encouraging Sarah to work toward. Sally visited more often than I did. When I did stop by, the residents were always sitting in the dark, watching TV. Sarah spent most of her time alone in her room, watching movies and listening to Broadway shows. She never complained.

"It's not an interview," Sally said. "They just want to get an idea of who she is."

It seemed that RSI was vetting potential residents, which I found reassuring. The possibility that Sarah might not make the cut was less so. I wondered if there was anything we could do to increase her odds of getting in.

"I can't imagine Sarah having a problem," Sally said. "She gets along with most everyone."

She was right. Sarah had sparkle. Even back in elementary school, when I walked with her down the hallway, teachers, students, the principal, everyone called her name and waved. I was walking beside a celebrity.

"When?" I rinsed the plates and put them in the dishwasher. If the new group home in Chapel Hill was like the one we had toured ten years previously, it would be a huge upgrade.

———

A few days later, we went to Sarah's group home in Durham to pick her up. The young woman with the clammy hands answered the door. "Sarah," she yelled. "Your mom and dad are here."

Sally and I stepped inside. The odor wasn't bad, just a little musty. I wondered how it seemed to Sarah. When I'd asked her if she liked living there, she'd said, "Not really."

Sarah turned sideways to slip past her housemate standing right in the middle of hallway. Sarah looked me in the eyes and raised her eyebrows as if to say, *See what it's like?*

The group home manager asked when we'd be back. I felt like we were ditching them, the way one might feel if offered a chance to move to first class on a packed flight: most of us would appreciate more leg room, but we might feel a twinge of guilt at leaving behind the people buckled into the cramped seats.

"Couple of hours," Sally said. "We're going to have supper while we're out."

"Good," Sarah said. "Chick-fil-A?"

As we drove away, I noticed that the yard next door still had a rusted-out grill lying on its side. The house three doors down still had two red Firebirds up on blocks.

Sally gave directions. I drove. Sarah sat in the back seat. Usually she was chatty. Today she was quiet. Sally had told her she might be moving to a different group home.

"You okay?" I asked, looking up into the rearview mirror. She nodded.

"Excited?

"Sort of."

Our van remained uncharacteristically quiet on the twenty-minute drive over to Chapel Hill.

"This must be it," Sally said.

The lawns were carefully landscaped, shaded with large, old trees. No sagging gutters. No cars up on cinderblocks.

"Just behind the van," Sally said. I pulled in close to the granite curb.

The group home had gray siding and white trim. A bed of glossy green liriope was tucked in under a small magnolia tree, the leaves waxy and dark. The front yard rose steeply up from the street, and tall pine trees shaded the house.

Sarah climbed out of the van and looked around.

The driveway up to the house was steep. Sarah, Sally, and I walked slowly.

"What do you think?" Sally asked.

"It's nice." Sarah's voice was soft.

The house had just been remodeled, and the space was open and light and airy. Sunlight streamed through windows lining a hallway that led to the room addition in the back. The front room had a dining area, a TV area, and a large kitchen. The walls were white in the living room, yellow in the kitchen. Down the hallway another, smaller area had a TV. Movie posters from *Singing in the Rain* and *Breakfast at Tiffany's* were framed and hanging on walls that were painted a rich burgundy. The hardwood floors had a natural finish.

We met several of Sarah's prospective housemates. A thin young man with a brace on his wrist told us that he loved UNC basketball. A young woman told us about her job at a nursing home. She was able to drive, and hoped to get her own apartment. Another young woman was tall, direct, and had a quick laugh. They all seemed about Sarah's age, and high-functioning. They seemed glad to meet Sarah.

The staff member was an undergraduate at UNC who

planned to go to medical school. She wanted to become a psychiatrist for people with intellectual disabilities. She showed Sarah the room that would be hers, if everything worked out. It was a corner room, and had two windows.

———

"Wow," Sarah said as she clicked her seatbelt in place.

I pulled the van away from the curb.

"Do you think I can move, Mom?" Her voice sounded happier than it had in months.

"I hope so," Sally said. She looked at me and crossed her fingers.

A few days later, when I got home from work, Sally met me at the door.

"RSI called," Sally said. "She got in." Sally spread her arms for a hug.

Simple as that.

The move was cheerful, at least after we pulled out of the cul-de-sac in front of the old group home, the truck lurching slightly, the pink entertainment center swaying. Sarah's new room was a pale and pleasant green. It went well with her bedspread and a pink street sign with white letters: "Princess Way." Sarah asked that I put it above her bed.

I looked forward to picking Sarah up to go to the movies. I loved the light-filled spaces in the new group home,
and her housemates who always asked what movie we were
going to see, and said that they'd seen the trailer and it
looked like a good one. As Sarah and I walked through the
front door, they'd call out to tell us to have a good time.
And I enjoyed the tree-lined street, and the bustle of activity
that seemed always to be going on—a staff member and a
resident washing dinner dishes, or the van pulling up from
a trip to Target. Sarah seemed happier. Her teeth always
looked brushed and her hair recently washed. Her dandruff
got better. "There are consequences," Sarah explained to
me. "If you don't cooperate." She listed on her fingers, "You
have to help cook, or clean up afterward. Brush your teeth.
Wash your hair. Wash and dry your clothes."

"What are the consequences?" I asked.

"I don't know," Sarah said. "But I don't want them."

Chapter Twenty-Two

Sarah and I were in the car, going out to dinner and a movie. While we were waiting for a traffic light to change, NPR began a segment on the "R word." *Retarded.* The piece was about a crusade to classify the word as hate speech, and to replace it with the term "intellectually disabled." A father of a girl with Down syndrome was being interviewed, and told of the time he was yelling at a person who had cut him off in traffic: "And I actually said that word, and then I stopped the car and got teary, and I thought, Oh my gosh, I can't believe I just said that."

Sarah, twenty-two, was sitting in the passenger seat, her pocketbook on the floor between her feet. Her lips moved as she had a silent conversation with herself. She didn't seem to hear the radio.

Retarded. It's a word that'll get the hackles up. Of course, it's better than "idiot," "moron," "imbecile," and "feeble-minded," all of which were coined as medical terms—technical terms—each one designating a specific IQ range. Over time, popular culture coopted the words, until the Three Stooges used them as often as eye-pokes and dope-slaps.

We've been converting medical terms into terms of derision for over a century. In 1887, John Langdon Down gave a series of lectures to the Medical Society of London. "The gradations of mental incapacity are as numerous and delicate as those of mental capacity among those who are doing the world's work. The division, therefore, into imbeciles and idiots is thoroughly wrong and misleading. I have no great liking for the term idiot. It is so frequently the name of reproach."[50] He goes on to say, "The term idiot might be advantageously replaced by that of feeble-minded, idiocy being in fact mental feebleness depending on malnutrition or disease of the nervous centres taking place anterior to birth or during the developmental years of childhood and youth." He was unsuccessful in his attempt to purge the term "idiot" from the medical literature, and in fact used it when defining the "mongolian" type of idiocy, which has since been renamed Down syndrome or trisomy 21.[51]

The term "mental retardation" was initially used as a purely medical term. But in the 1960s it, too, became a term of derision.

The National Down Syndrome Society prefers "intellectual disability" over "mental retardation," and I have heard parents of Down syndrome use the term "developmentally delayed," a term I've used in the past. I feel an inward cringe when I hear "mentally retarded," which sounds almost as bad as "feeble-minded," but both terms seem more honest than "developmentally delayed," which implies that if we all work hard enough, and wait long enough, Sarah will "get there." But Sarah knows that no matter how diligently she works, she will always have Down syndrome. She will never "catch up."

It seems that even the most carefully formulated nomenclature will eventually be corrupted: the term "special" has been turned into a singsong taunt on school yard playgrounds. I wonder how long it will take for "intellectual disability" to sound as antiquated and pejorative as "feeble-minded."

"They don't know how it feels," Sam said one day after school. He was twelve. A quick and physical kid, Sam would rather jump than worry about where he was going to land. One of his buddies had been imitating a "retard" while everyone laughed.

"I wanted to punch him out." Sam sat forward, face set, his eyes glistening with tears. "They've got no idea what it's like."

Sally was proud that he didn't hit the kid.

I was proud that he wanted to.

—

The car's radio continued with the story of the dad who had yelled the R word and subsequently started an "anti–R word campaign." He wanted to have the word "retarded" bleeped from television shows, and had written letters to every commissioner of the FCC, the President of the United States, and even Oprah. I wondered if he wasn't taking it a bit far: I mean, he had used the word himself with his intellectually disabled daughter sitting right behind him.

It's not a word I've used in traffic. I've muttered "asshole" when another driver has cut me off. There are lots of other words I'm not proud of using. On the occasions that Sarah has heard me curse, she laughed loudly and said, "Busted!!!" smacking her palm against her thigh, turning to see if anyone has witnessed her catching me using crude language.

The word "retarded" blurted out of the radio speakers a few more times. I glanced over at Sarah. She appeared oblivious.

"What do you think?" I asked her.

She startled. "What?"

"What do you think about this?" I pointed toward the radio.

"I wasn't listening."

"It's about the word 'retarded.'"

"Oh." She looked at the car's radio, and didn't say anything.

"Does it bother you?" I asked.

"It depends," she said, her voice matter-of-fact. "If a staff member says it, that's one thing." She turned toward me, and frowned. "But if someone says, 'you retard,' that's different." Her voice sounded scornful when she said "retard."

"Fair enough," I said. The car behind me honked. I glanced at the traffic light. It was green. We drove a few blocks without talking. I was proud that Sarah could tease out the nuances of language, but I wondered if something so hurtful could really be so cut and dried.

"It's a stereotype," she said at the next traffic light. "And it's mean."

Chapter Twenty-Three

Sarah, her mother, and I were sitting together, waiting for the talent show to begin. John and Sam had decided not to join us. Our seats were in the middle of a lecture hall at the University of North Carolina. Down in the front, a stage extended across the entire width of the room. Large blue lettering filled an erasable board: "WELCOME TO THE BEST BUDDIES TALENT SHOW—IF YOU ARE PERFORMING, PLEASE SIGN IN AT THE DESK." Two members of the sorority that sponsored Best Buddies sat at a folding table on the far left side of the stage.

"So, what are you going to do?" I asked Sarah.

She was twenty-two, but looked closer to thirteen or fourteen. "You'll see."

"But is it dancing, or singing, or what?"

"Dad," she said, shaking her head. "You'll see." The waves of her blond hair caught the light, and fell down in front of her shoulders and chest. Her bangs, which she'd been growing out, swooped down over her eyebrow.

She was wearing a red T-shirt with a winter scene of two penguins ice-skating beneath puffy white clouds.

"Is it about penguins?"

"Oh, brother." She turned to Sally and gestured toward me with her thumb. "Here we go again." She shook her head. "It isn't about penguins. It's the only red shirt I had. To go with my dress." Sarah's skirt was a patchwork of patterns: gingham, plaid, and a floral print with red hibiscus blossoms.

Sally looked down at the program the college girl had handed her at the door. "There are a lot of performers," she said.

Sarah nodded. "We're near the last."

"How far down?" I asked. Sally turned the page over.

Sarah placed a finger near the bottom of that page. "Here's Ramseur." Sarah's group home was on Ramseur Road in Chapel Hill. She'd been there a couple of years. The Ramseur house was for high-functioning young adults: four females and two males. Four of them would be performing in the talent show. They were all sitting in the front row. Sarah had come back into the audience to sit with us.

"Did you sign in?" I asked Sarah.

"Yes, Dad."

I glanced at my watch. Ten minutes after two. It was scheduled to start at two.

A cluster of people paused at the door, and then strag-
gled in. The first young woman had erect posture and
moved quickly. Behind her was a woman whose right foot
pointed inward. She had a shuffling, syncopated gait, and
I felt myself flinch with each of her steps, as if to catch her
if she fell. Holding her hand was a heavyset young woman
with straggly brown hair.

Behind these two women was a stocky man with Down
syndrome, dressed all in black: jeans, shirt, and a cowboy
hat. The staff member led them to the desk at the far left of
the stage to check in. I looked at my watch again. Quarter
past. At two thirty, the sorority sister with the long blond hair
walked to center stage and welcomed us to the talent show.

———

A willowy woman with red cheeks sang "I Will Always
Love You." She seemed shy, and tucked her chin against
her chest. Her movements were stiff and mechanical—
unrelated to beat, or melody, or lyrics. Her voice was hushed
and breathy. When she was done she waved to her friends.
They whooped and cheered for her.

Next, a woman with gray hair cut as short as a man's
shuffled to center stage. Drop pearl earrings dangled beside
her ropy neck. Michael Jackson's "Black Or White" boomed

out of the speakers. The woman's voice was so soft I could not hear her. Her lips moved, but the rest of her body was absolutely motionless. When the song was done, she shuffled offstage to polite applause.

As I clapped, I glanced around at the audience, mostly people from group homes and staff members, and the sorority sisters who organized the talent show. I nodded and smiled with whoever made eye contact—usually other "regular people"—family members, staff, sitting quietly. The others talked, called out encouragement, and laughed unself-consciously. Across the aisle from me, a young woman bobbed her head rhythmically, ceaselessly. Her fingers were stiff and waved independently.

Two other people performed Michael Jackson's "Black Or White." Two different groups danced to "We Are Family" by Sister Sledge.

———

Sarah's turn. She walked down to the stage, settled a silver plastic tiara on her head, and put on a blue plaid lumberjack shirt. I followed her to the front of the room and sat on the floor, so I could take pictures.

She had a feather boa, as black as ink. Sarah lifted the center of the boa, and settled it over her head. The fluff of feathers draped down the sides of her face, down in front of her breasts, down past her waist, almost to her knees. The boa was thick and extravagant and lush; it enveloped her face, until all that could be seen were the cut glass gems of the tiara—white diamonds, red rubies—and her eyes and nose. Sarah's face was tilted upward, eyes closed.

The blue plaid shirt was unbuttoned and open, showing the red T-shirt with the skating penguins. Under her patchwork skirt she was wearing black tights. At the ankles, the tights were stuffed down into hot pink socks. The socks bulged with the lump of the fabric.

Sarah waited, her hands at her side, fingers in a relaxed curve. She looked small and vulnerable, standing so still. Sparkles from the rhinestones glinted though the raven-black feathers. If this were New York, and if Sarah didn't have Down syndrome, I would see this as conceptual art. Avant-garde. Something Yoko Ono might do, for an audience of skinny, humorless people who don't get out in the sun often enough.

The music started with a few repeated notes on a piano, and then a distorted percussion cadence that buzzed and rattled the speakers, a techno beat with a heavy bass line thumping urgently.

Lady Gaga. "Poker Face."

With her eyes still closed, Sarah moved her arms to the

music, and then whipped the boa from her head and twirled it like a lasso, and then let go. The boa seemed to float in midair for a few seconds before drifting to the floor, as Sarah whirled in the opposite direction. She thrust her hips to the beat, and then opened her eyes and moved both hands to the sides of the tiara, pulled it off, and flung it like a Frisbee toward the audience. She thrashed her head right and then left, her long blond hair trailing as if blown in a hurricane. She pumped her arms, keeping beat with the driving bass, while Lady Gaga sang about how hot she'd get her lover.

Sarah yanked her plaid shirt off. Her feet spread wide, she twirled the shirt and whipped it off to the side.

Wow. I snapped a picture.

The young man next to me jumped to his feet, clapping and screaming, stomping his foot. I couldn't make out what he was shouting, over and over, but I thought it was "Yeah, baby."

I kept taking pictures with my small instamatic camera.

Sarah threw her left shoulder forward, her left hand on her left knee, dipped down, and then straightened and twirled, her hair swirling out. She stopped, her stance wide, arms back, and threw her chest forward, pumping her arms. The speakers rattled and buzzed with the urgency of rough love as Lady Gaga sang of games with guns and rolling with her lover.

Sarah dropped to the floor, rolled to the left, then the right, her hair a blur of curls. On her back, she did three hip thrusts, and then she got up on her hands and knees, shaking her head from side to side with the music.

The young man next to me was jumping up and down, and I heard someone yell, "Go, Sarah, go."

I continued snapping pictures.

Sarah stood, took off one shoe, threw it out to the crowd, made a pumping move with her hips, took off the other shoe, and threw it forward as well. She then shifted her hips right and left, giving them a snap that made her hair shake.

The young man next to me howled a baying sound, and Lady Gaga's music kept thumping.

Sarah bent forward at the waist, swirled her torso, her hair propelling in a blond storm of swirls. The song wound down to its final chorus.

Sarah stood, smiled, and waved as the crowd erupted in applause, people yelling her name, howling, and whistling. Sarah waved again, the noise increased, and she walked off the stage as the yelps and whoops continued.

"Suzette, you're next," the Ramseur Road staff member said to one of Sarah's housemates. She had to pitch her voice loudly to be heard over the audience.

"I'm not going up there," she said, shaking her head. "Not after that."

I stood, and went back to sit with Sally and Sarah. Sarah's face was flushed and had a faint sheen of sweat.

"Good job," I whispered, wondering if we were going to get in trouble.

"Thanks," she whispered back.

I only half watched the other performances. A young woman wearing a yellow T-shirt with stripes of black duct tape sang along to a children's song, "I'm Bringing Home a Baby Bumblebee," to a recording of a toy piano. Another of Sarah's housemates, Jerry, danced to the song, "Oops, I Did it Again," the chorus of which is "I'm not that innocent." I was starting to feel a little better. Maybe Sarah was just expressing what most of the young adults were feeling. She sure got more whoops, yells, and applause than the Bumblebee girl.

After the show, one of Sarah's staff members walked up the aisle toward us. Here we go. She's going to tell Sarah that her dance was inappropriate and sexually suggestive. She's going to be talking to Sarah, but meaning it for Sally and me, for raising a child who would mistake a talent show for a strip club.

"My Lady Gaga." The staff member opened her arms for a hug. "Sarah, you were great!"

Sarah hugged her back.

"Wasn't she wonderful?" the staff member said to Sally and me. "I mean, she just burned it up."

On the way to the car, I asked her about the boa draped across her head.

"I was doing Snow White," Sarah says. "She has black hair. I couldn't afford a wig."

"And throwing the crown away?"

"It was symbolic."

Oh. "And taking off the shoes and throwing them?"

"That was about dealing with anger."

Chapter Twenty-Four

When Sarah tossed her black feather boa to the floor and her tiara into the crowd, she was expressing a new version of herself. It must have felt good to dance so freely, after so many years of being constrained by the expectations of others.

People with intellectual disabilities rarely get to tell the rest of us how they see themselves. When they do speak up, parents, teachers, and caregivers often ignore what they say: we've already decided who they are, and what's best for them.

Peter Singer, a bioethicist, believes it would be best if parents of "defective infants" were able to euthanize them in the first weeks of life. Doubting the accuracy of the quote, I looked at his website, where he conceded that he had written, "Killing a defective infant is not morally equivalent to killing a person. Sometimes it is not wrong at all." He went on to say that the quote could be misleading if read without the understanding of what he meant by "person."[52] Apparently, Singer had found a way to define "person" in such a way that it's okay to kill a "defective" one.

After reading the history of the treatment of people with disabilities, I could understand why Hitler would try to kill everyone who was deaf or blind and those with schizophrenia, Huntington's chorea, or an intellectual disability; Hitler was nuts. His neck veins bulged as he screamed into the microphone and jabbed his fingers into the air.

But what about Singer? He didn't seem insane. On the contrary, some of his peers called him the most widely read and influential of modern philosophers.[53] But how likely is it that his ideas of "life unworthy of living" would really take hold again in popular culture, as they did in the United States and Germany in the 1920s and 1930s?

In 2005, *Time* magazine named Singer one of the 100 most influential people in the world. In that article, Arthur Caplan, PhD, the director of the Center for Bioethics at the University of Pennsylvania, said, "It is easy to demonize Singer, 58, since his theory points toward conclusions that some find morally repugnant—for example, that euthanasia might be the appropriate response to the intractable suffering of an infant born with a terrible genetic malady. Those who scorn his views can rarely produce an argument about why he is wrong—they simply don't like his conclusions. But ethics is all about arguments, not moral pronouncements."[54]

I knew that I would never win a philosophical debate with Singer: it's his full-time job, and he's good at it. But even if I knew I'd lose an argument with him, I thought that I should at least read his books: he was talking about killing people like Sarah.

———

The title of *Practical Ethics* is printed in chunky, bold italics. A small paperback, it would be a tight squeeze in the back pocket of a pair of jeans, but could easily get lost in the bottom of a knapsack. Printed by a university press, the book is used in philosophy classes and ethics seminars.

I picked up a copy from a used bookstore. On the facing page of the inside cover, a student had written her name with ballpoint pen in careful, left-slanted cursive. Underneath she had written "Philosophy 100." Sitting at the kitchen table, I glanced through the marginal notes she had made in her dutiful script, and then looked at the brown and orange cover. I thumbed through the book again, and set it down.

I picked it up, and glanced over the table of contents. What if I failed to frame an adequate argument? Worse still, what if I agreed with some of the things he said?

Singer's writing was clear and engaging, and the tone conversational. In the first lines, he said that he used the terms "ethics" and "morality" interchangeably. He went on to say that morality was not a "system of nasty puritanical prohibitions, mainly designed to stop people having fun." Further, ethics was not an "ideal system, which is all very noble in theory, but no good in practice. The reverse of this is closer to the truth: an ethical judgment that is of no good in practice must suffer from a theoretical defect as well, for the whole point of ethical judgment is to guide practice."[55] Singer wasn't involved in a theoretical exercise: if I understood him correctly, he wasn't puritanical, he had no objection to having fun, and he really wanted to kill disabled children.

I read a few chapters, and then put the book down. I knew he was wrong, but didn't think I'd be able to prove it. I wished I could do what Samuel Johnson did when confronted with a logical argument that was wrong but irrefutable. As Boswell reported in his *Life of Samuel Johnson*:

> After we came out of the church, we stood talking for some time together of Bishop Berkeley's ingenious sophistry to prove the nonexistence of matter, and that every thing in the universe is merely ideal. I observed, that though we are satisfied his doctrine is not true, it is impossible to refute it. I never shall forget the alacrity with which Johnson answered, striking his foot with mighty force against a large stone, till he rebounded from it—"I refute it *thus*."[56]

What rock could I kick to prove Singer wrong? Could I place Sarah in front of him, as proof that her life was, in fact, worth living? The thought of his cold stare pausing on the soft contours of Sarah's face made my stomach queasy. But what if we took a jury of Sarah's peers with us, to even things up? Let them discuss if *his* life was worth living. If *he* should be allowed to live. The only problem with this strategy is that Sarah's housemates would laugh and say, "Of *course* he should be allowed to live." Then they'd invite him back to the group home for dinner.

I picked the book up again, and settled into the job. It was slow work. I made note cards, hoping to find a fault in his logic. At the end of the day, I flipped through the fragments of thoughts:

Snails and newborns have no desires for the future.

Killing robs autonomy.

Some nonhuman animals are persons.

Some members of other species are persons: some members of our own species are not.

We can rank value of different lives.

Killing a chimp is worse than killing a defective person.

I found his conclusions repugnant, but, as Dr. Caplan had predicted, I could find no fault in his logic. I paged back though the book looking for a chink: Singer hammered at "defective persons" and the "severely retarded" and the "mentally defective" over and over, page after page.

His logic was as hard and implacable as the cast-iron linkage of railroad cars. Boxcar by boxcar, he built his argument: if a recently fused sperm and egg are not a "human," and if a two-day-old blob of cells is not "human," why is a fetus at twenty weeks a "human," but not at nineteen weeks? It's arbitrary, really, when we can or cannot get an abortion. And if it's okay to get an abortion at twenty weeks, why not at thirty, or forty? And if okay at forty weeks, why not in the first few days, or weeks, of life?

I could not argue with the logic. And I could not deny that Sally and I would have aborted a twelve-week fetus with a genetic disease. I was stuck.

Singer did not shy away from taking every argument to its radical, unsettling conclusion: "Some members of other species are persons: some members of our species are not . . . So it seems that killing, say, a chimpanzee is worse than killing a gravely defective human who is not a person." He also wrote, "If defective newborn infants were not regarded as having a right to life until, say, a week or a month after birth, it would allow us to choose on the basis of a far greater knowledge of the infant's condition than is possible before birth."

In spite of myself, I felt a grudging respect for the rigor of his logic and for his intellectual courage. But on further reflection, his intellectual courage seemed nothing more than a pose, an illusion: if he followed the argument all the way to the end, he would tell us what he would propose *after* killing a "gravely defective human who is not a person." Would he suggest a funeral service with a casket, cemetery, and gravestone, or would it be a backyard affair with a cardboard box?

At the Hartheim Euthanasia Center in Alkoven, Austria, between 1940 and 1941, the National Socialist Party euthanized 18,269 persons with intellectual disabilities. The staff at the center dealt with the bodies in a straightforward manner: workers walked into the gas chamber, untangled the naked bodies, loaded them into an oven, and then carted the ashes and bits of bone to the Danube River and shoveled them in. The burning of bodies was done during the day. The dumping of ashes was done at night. When they fired up the furnaces, women in the town would rush out and take down any laundry they had out on the line to dry, to keep the ashes that floated down from the black and oily smoke from staining their clothes.[57]

Paragraph after paragraph and page after page, Singer built the justification for killing "defective humans" and the "mentally retarded" and the "hopelessly retarded." His logic was blunt and relentless.

What if Singer met an adult who, as an infant, would have met his criteria for infanticide? And what if the person he would have deemed "defective" had grown up and gone to law school? Would Singer say, "Gosh. Maybe I was wrong."?

Don't bet on it. As Harriet McBryde Johnson, a disability rights attorney, wrote in the *New York Times Magazine*, Singer wasn't swayed:

> He insists he doesn't want to kill me. He simply thinks it would have been better, all things considered, to have given my parents the option of killing the baby I once was, and to let other parents kill similar babies as they come along and thereby avoid the suffering that comes with lives like mine and satisfy the reasonable preferences of parents for a different kind of child. It has nothing to do with me. I should not feel threatened.
>
> He proceeds with the assumption that I am one of the people who might rightly have been killed at birth. He sticks to his guns, conceding just enough to show himself open-minded and flexible. We go back and forth for 10 long minutes. Even as I am horrified by what he says, and by the fact that I have been sucked into a civil discussion of whether I ought to exist, I can't help being dazzled by his verbal facility.[58]

I remembered a line in the novel *Get Shorty*, by Elmore Leonard, in which Chili Palmer told Harry, another man with frizzy hair and a bald spot, "You're trying to tell me how you fucked up without sounding stupid." Or maybe Dr. Singer really could not see that he had been mistaken, even after his debate with such a vibrant and intelligent woman—a woman he would have killed as an infant.

It must be hard to admit you've said something stupid when you've become such a celebrity for being so smart.

In his book *Rethinking Life and Death: The Collapse of Our Traditional Ethics*, Singer discussed Down syndrome. "We cannot expect a child with Down syndrome to play the guitar, to develop an appreciation of science fiction, to learn a foreign language, to chat with us about the latest Woody Allen movie, or to be a respectable athlete, basketball or tennis player." He goes on to say, "Both for the sake of 'our children,' then, and for our own sake, we may not want a child to start on life's uncertain voyage if the prospects are clouded."

Woody Allen? This is a make-or-break point that Singer would choose between those who should be allowed to live and those who shouldn't? My daughter Sarah does, in fact, love to talk about her favorite movies. She's a bigger fan of Meryl Streep than Woody Allen, but then so am I.

I put Singer's *Practical Ethics* down. Dr. Arthur Caplan was right: I could find no weakness in Singer's argument, no

Achilles heel. Then it occurred to me: the flaw wasn't in what he had put into the book; it was what he had left out. Singer made no reference to the things that most of us associate with humanity. He made no mention of touch. Warmth. Understanding. Humility. No mention of the possibility of being wrong, or of forgiveness. There were no crooked smiles, no sideways glances. No humor. No music. There was no mention of being cherished by a sister or brother, lover, or friend. All of the relationships in *Practical Ethics* were between ideas, not people.

Sarah and I had no answer to the cold precision of Singer's logic. It is not surprising; Singer is smarter than Sarah and me put together. And Sarah and I both would rather write a story than build an argument. Sarah doesn't write as well as I do, but I don't dance as well as she does.

Chapter Twenty-Five

Sarah leaned toward me, pulling her car door shut. "I know you don't like musicals," she said as she twisted around to grab her shoulder belt. "That's why I suggested a romantic comedy." We had just seen a movie about a bounty hunter taking his ex-wife back to jail.

"Good call," I said. I put the key in the ignition. "But I like just about everything else. Except horror." We went to the movies every couple of months or so. She picked the movie. I drove. Sarah's group home was about twenty minutes from our house. She didn't have a driver's license. She was working on getting privileges to ride on a city bus by herself.

"I like comedies," she said. "I like dramas. I like romance. I like romantic comedies, action, Disney, suspense, and musicals." She took a deep breath. "I like 'em all."

At the climax of the movie we'd just watched, the heroine, a lithe young journalist in a close-fitting turtleneck, racked a shell into a shotgun and fired a warning shot over the villain's head. Her recently reconciled husband then

punched the guy right in the nuts. This movie had something for everybody.

"You're a good movie buddy," I said. John, nineteen, and
Sam, sixteen, would sometimes watch a TV show with me.
But they wouldn't go to movies with me.

"Yup." Sarah gripped her lower lip between her teeth and
buckled her seatbelt.

————

Sometimes, when we stepped up to the ticket window to
buy two adult tickets to the latest romantic comedy, I felt
a little self-conscious. It might have appeared that I was
taking a grade-school kid to a movie with a trailer that
showed a mother-in-law slinking around in fishnet stock-
ings and leering at her son-in-law. But, Sarah was, in fact,
twenty-two. And she picked the movies.

We always stopped at the concessions stand and Sarah
always got a small combo—Diet Coke and popcorn. In the
theater, she sat patiently with the popcorn bag on her lap.
She didn't eat a kernel, didn't take a sip, until the movie
began. Not the trailers. Not the opening titles. She waited
for the movie itself.

I was often surprised at how much I enjoyed the movies that Sarah chose. Some of the detective buddy films she

picked out I would have otherwise skipped, and some of the screwball comedies reached for laughs that were too predictable. But the movie itself didn't matter so much as sitting in the dark beside my daughter and hearing her laugh without restraint. If her laughter was sometimes too loud or sounded forced, if it was a little off-key or lagged behind everyone else's, who cared?

When I glanced over, Sarah's face would be lit from the screen, and fully engaged in the movie. We gave each other a fist bump when we saw a trailer that we were both interested in.

We usually went out for supper beforehand, and Sarah told me about her job bagging groceries at Harris Teeter, and about the residents and staff at the group home. Sarah's stories were intricate, and full of energy and emotion: customers who got impatient at the grocery store, who told her to hurry up bagging the groceries.

"It's like the time I started crying at a Winnie-the-Pooh movie," Sarah said. We were at a traffic light, on the way home from the romantic comedy about the bounty hunter and his bail-jumping ex-wife.

I glanced at her, and then back at the red traffic light.

"You cried at a Winnie-the-Pooh movie?" Sarah's conversation could skip off into a non sequitur pretty quickly, and I'd learned to reflect back what she'd just said, with the hope of finding a track I could follow.

"They were throwing popcorn at me."

"Who?"

"The other kids. They laughed at me. Called me 'retard.'"

"During a Winnie-the-Pooh movie?" The light turned green and I pulled away from the intersection. "When was this?"

"At a party," she said. "A birthday party."

"Your birthday?" I couldn't remember a time we'd taken her to a Winnie-the-Pooh movie party, but working rotating shifts, I missed out on a lot of my family's life.

"No," she said. "A different kid's birthday."

Sometimes it was difficult to tell if Sarah was accurately reporting a factual event. When she got to the intersection of memory and imagination, she rarely paused before barreling along with her story. Once, when Sarah was in high school, her special-ed teacher asked my wife if we had enjoyed our Christmas trip to Italy. Sally told her that we've never been to Europe. "Are you sure?" the teacher said. "Sarah told us about the Sistine Chapel, and everything. Her descriptions were so vivid!" Sally laughed and said, "No, I'd remember a family vacation to Italy."

"When was this party?" I asked.

"I forget." Sarah looked over at me. "But they were laughing at me. Throwing popcorn. Calling me 'retard.'"

"That sounds terrible," I said. "What did you do?"

"Mom took me out of that theater, and we went into another one to see a different movie."

I nodded, and kept driving. That didn't sound like something Sally would do. I could imagine Sally suggesting that Sarah move back a few rows. I could see her telling the other kids to stop. I could see her taking Sarah home. But somehow, I couldn't see Sally and Sarah ducking into a different movie.

"Maybe it was Karen Brown," Sarah said. "Remember her? The babysitter?"

"Yes," I said. I remembered the name, but couldn't picture her. There was one with a tattoo of a dolphin on her left ankle, but her name wasn't Karen. Sally would know which one Karen was. She still exchanged Christmas cards with some of the young women who babysat Sarah twenty years ago. Sally still got graduation announcements and wedding announcements from former babysitters. She smiled when she referred to them as her surrogate daughters.

Sally had also found other surrogates. She'd recently begun to enjoy her role as an aunt. Watching her nieces develop was painful for the first ten years or so. Each milestone a niece achieved just underscored how delayed Sarah was. But, for reasons neither of us understood, when the girls hit adolescence, Sally was able to enjoy watching them grow up. Talk about boyfriends, college plans.

"Karen Brown was with me," Sarah said. "She took me to go see a different movie. I forget what it was."

"Oh." The story was losing plausibility with each new detail. I grew up listening to stories my dad told—stories about Oklahoma during the Depression. The Dust Bowl. A prison guard for a dad. The stories were all shaped and smoothed from being told over and over. Subtle variations and flourishes were understood to be part of the point.

I didn't know what to do with the Winnie-the-Pooh popcorn-throwing story, other than listen. I would probably never know if, in fact, some kid did or didn't throw popcorn at Sarah, years ago.

"That's too bad," I said. "I always liked Winnie-the-Pooh." As a child, I sat for hours leafing through the book, staring at the pen-and-ink drawings of Pooh clutching a honey jar at the door at the base of the tree, Pooh and Piglet leaving footprints in the snow, Pooh stuck halfway in and halfway out a rabbithole.

"Not me," Sarah said.

The needle of my gas gauge crossed into the red zone and I pulled into a minimart. "Need gas."

"I like all kinds of movies," Sarah said, her voice rising. "Action movies, drama movies, romantic comedies, Disney movies, musicals, even horror movies." Her tone had become adamant and angry. Like a TV preacher getting wound up, Sarah's tone scaled upward. She leaned toward me. Speaking slowly and distinctly, she enunciated each word for emphasis. "But I don't like Winnie-the-Pooh."

I had my door open, and was about to step outside.

"It isn't just the popcorn, either," she said, leaning back and folding her arms over her chest.

I waited for her to go on.

"Go ahead," she said. "Pump the gas."

"It won't take but a sec."

She shrugged her shoulders, her arms still locked over each other.

As the numbers on the pump flicked past and the gas sluiced into the car, I looked in at Sarah through the back window. Sometimes, when she got going, it was hard for her to stop. And sometimes it seemed that she didn't know where she was going with it.

The nozzle clicked off.

As we pulled into traffic, Sarah said, "It was Karen Brown."

"Okay," I said. Her voice still sounded angry, and I wasn't sure if she was mad at the kids who threw popcorn years ago, or if she had registered the fact that I had doubted parts of her story. Maybe she was just in a bad mood. I hoped not. We had both enjoyed our movie date.

We drove silently.

"People blame the actors," Sarah said. "But they shouldn't."

"Blame them for what?" I asked, still wondering where this conversation was going.

"Everything. If there's something they don't like about the movie, or something their kid sees that they think is inappropriate, they shouldn't blame the actor. They just say the lines they're given." Sarah had wanted to be a movie star ever since she was in middle school. Either that or a scriptwriter. "But people don't get it. It's the writers and producers and directors who make all the decisions."

"I bet you're right," I said.

"But people have dreams. And teenagers have dreams that their parents don't let them fulfill." Her arms were still crossed, and she was staring at me.

Oh. She was working around to how her dreams got crushed. It's a story she'd told me many times.

"Remember how I wanted to go to Hollywood, but you wouldn't let me?"

"We didn't stop you," I said.

"You put me in a group home."

"You were ready to move out." I looked over at her. "Or at least almost ready."

She looked away.

"And now you're in a great group home, with great housemates."

She conceded the point with a small shrug.

"Any time you want to take acting lessons, just let me know. I'll be glad to pay for them. Just like your dance lessons." Sally had danced ever since I've known her: over twenty-five years. Last year, one of Sally's teachers started a special needs dance class that Sarah attended once a week.

"Huh." She shook her head, and looked out at the ranch houses we were driving past.

We'd had this conversation before. Sarah had an ear for a good storyline, and liked to think that if her ambition hadn't been squashed, she'd already be in Hollywood. She was always telling me about movie ideas, and ideas for books. And as appealing an idea as it was—a young woman taking a Greyhound bus to Hollywood with nothing but a love of movies and a battered suitcase—it made for a better movie plot than career plan. Even for a young person who was not developmentally disabled. When Sarah showed interest in singing, Sally enrolled her in Voices Together, a local choral group for special needs adults. They gave a Christmas recital once a year, and Sarah read the introductions to some of the songs, and had an occasional solo. But she didn't want to take acting lessons or try out for local theater groups. She wanted to move to Hollywood, get discovered, and become a star in hit movies.

"It's not just the actors." Sarah had unclenched her arms,

and turned to face me. "Directors, producers, costume people," she said, gesturing with her hand. "People have no idea
of what's involved in making a movie."

"I bet that's true." I half expected her to talk about how
hard it is to line up the money.

We drove in silence the rest of the way.

She nodded and murmured a few words to herself. Ever
since she was an infant, Sarah had imaginary friends. She
had learned not to talk or laugh out loud during an imaginary conversation, but she often murmured to herself and
made small gestures with her hands.

I pulled into the driveway of her group home.

"Winnie-the-Pooh doesn't understand anything that's
going on around him," she said. "And all he cares about is
honey. It's his whole life." She snorted. "Honey." She unbuck-
led her seatbelt. "He's always having problems—even with
simple things." She looked me in the face. "Think about it:
He's a perfect symbol for people with special needs." She
leaned forward and snatched her pocketbook from the floor.
"And everybody laughs at him." She stepped out of the car.
Holding the door open, she said, "And that's why I don't
like Winnie-the-Pooh." She heaved the door shut with a sat-
isfying thwack, and trudged up the hill toward the group
home. She took short steps, and her arms swung side to side.

I pushed a button and my window slid silently down.

"Thanks for going to the movies with me," I called out. I couldn't tell if she was mad at me, or hurt by Winnie-the-Pooh, or satisfied that she had finally articulated something about a movie that had bugged her since she was in elementary school. "I had a great time," I called out.

She turned and waved, her palm toward me, fingers wide. The car's headlights made a blond nimbus of her hair. "Me too," she called back, smiling. Apparently, she wasn't mad at anybody. Then she was digging in her pocketbook, looking for her key to the front door.

Chapter Twenty-Six

I didn't know if Sarah would ever read this book. She hadn't read my first one. It was about the way my job in the emergency room almost wrecked my family. John and Sam haven't read the first book, either.

When I first started writing, Sally and I made a deal: I could write whatever I wanted without apology or explanation and she could delete whatever she wanted without apology or explanation. That way, I could write as honestly as possible and still stay married.

With this book, Sally had the same right to make deletions. I didn't, however, extend that prerogative to Sarah. On one hand, that decision seemed arbitrary: why shouldn't Sarah be able to edit her own story? On the other hand, Sally and I had exercised our best judgment in all aspects of Sarah's life since she was born, and continued to do so.

Although I didn't want to give Sarah final editorial authority, I did want to give her the chance to have her say before the book was published. By the time it was nearly finished, she had been in the second group home for sev-

eral years. Like one brother in college, and the other in the
Army, Sarah came home for a week or so every Christmas.
During the holidays, I printed a copy of the manuscript,
took it to Kinko/FedEx and had it spiral-bound.

When I got home, Sarah was on the front porch, swing-
ing high and singing loudly. I stood a few feet away. She
pulled her earphones down around her neck, and waited.

"You know the book I'm writing?" I asked. "With you
in it?"

"Yeah?"

"Here it is." I gave her a copy of the initial draft. It was
about an inch and a half thick. "Would you like to read it?"

"I don't know." She continued pumping with her legs.

"I'll just leave it here," I said. I put it on the small round
table under the mailbox. "If you decide to read it, I'd like to
know what you think of it."

"I don't know," she repeated. "We'll see."

The next time I went out onto the porch, the manuscript
was gone.

Two mornings later, I was pouring coffee for Sally and
me. Sarah walked into the kitchen. "Good morning, favorite daughter," I said.

Usually, Sarah would laugh, and say, "I'm your only
daughter." Then I'd say, "But you're still my favorite daughter," and she'd repeat "But I'm your *only* daughter," and
laugh again.

This morning, she didn't say anything.

"You okay?" I asked.

"I don't feel like joking around," she said. She poured a bowl of cereal without looking at me.

"Are you usually grumpy when you wake up?" I remembered her as cheerful in the mornings.

"Not really." She added milk, her movements slow and deliberate.

"What's wrong?"

"I read your book."

I pulled out the chair next to hers, and sat.

"It's long," she said. "I was up till 11:30."

I waited. "Anything else?"

"You don't think I'm a human." She turned and looked at me in the eyes.

"What?"

"That's what you said." She didn't blink. "In your book."

"Oh, no, Sarah. I didn't say that at all."

"Yes you did. In your book."

"I didn't write it very clearly, if that's what you think."

"And you said you didn't want me." Her voice was calm, her gaze unwavering.

"No, Sarah, no." I touched her shoulder. "That's not at all what I said in the book."

"It's how it seemed."

"No, sweetheart. The Down syndrome has been hard at times, but you've been great."

She turned her face away.

"I am sorry." I waited.

"Was Mommy smoking when I was born?" She turned to look at me again.

"What?"

"You said she was smoking. When I was born."

"Oh, the electrocautery pen. When they did the C-section, they had to cut through Sally's stomach, and there were some small blood vessels that were bleeding. They used an electric thing to burn them shut. That's where the smoke came from."

"Oh." She turned back to her cereal. "You can go now."

I carried the cooling cups of coffee to the bedroom, sat in bed with Sally, and told her about Sarah's response to the book.

"Do you think she read the whole thing?" Sally asked.

"I don't know. She said she did. Says she was up till 11:30."

"Wow."

Sarah walked into our bedroom. She climbed up onto the bed, and lay between Sally and me, facing Sally.

"Good morning again, favorite daughter," I said.

She didn't answer.

"Your father said good morning," Sally said.

Sarah shrugged.

"Were your feelings hurt by the book?" I asked.

She nodded.

"I can see that," I said. "There's a lot of hard stuff in there."

"Yeah," Sarah said. "About me not being human."

"Sarah," I said. "That wasn't me. That was John Locke, and Peter Singer. And I disagreed with both of them."

"It didn't seem like it."

"Do you know the F word?" I asked.

She turned partway to face me. "Do you mean 'fuck'?"

"Yeah, that's the one. In the book I said, 'Fuck John Locke.' That's how much I disagreed with him."

Sarah turned to face Sally again.

"The whole point of the book is that you're great but it took me a long time to see that."

Sarah scooted away from me, closer to her mother.

"In fact, you're going to be everyone's favorite character. Just like Sally was in my first book. Everyone's going to think that I was a crummy dad, but that you were great."

"Hah!" Sarah said. "You've got that right." Her back was still to me, but she didn't sound as hurt, or angry.

Sally looked over at me, and winked.

"Your book has too much Down syndrome in it," Sarah said.

"But Down syndrome is what your character has to overcome."

She turned halfway toward me.

"Cinderella is the hero of that story because she had to overcome all that washing and working and stuff. It wasn't about the stepsisters, because they didn't have to overcome anything. They already had it made."

Sarah was listening.

"I can just see it now," I said. "After the book comes out, customers are going to write reviews on Amazon, saying that I was cold and mean and that you were great."

"The wicked stepfather." She looked at me, and then away. "Hah!" Her tone was wry. "Good try, Dad."

"If they turn it into a movie" I said, "Who's going to play you?"

"I will," Sarah said, turning to face me again.

"Meryl Streep for Mom?" I asked.

"She can play herself. Johnny Depp can play you."

"Johnny Depp is going to be kissing my wife?" My voice scaled upward.

Sarah laughed. "No, Dad," she said. "In the movies, they kiss like this." She sat up, and softly cupped her palm across my lips. She kissed the back of her hand: her eyes open, looking into mine.

A few months later, Sarah and I were in the truck, on the way to a movie. This one was about a Civil war soldier who got teleported from a gold mine in Arizona right smack into the middle of a war on Mars.

"My editor agrees with you," I said.

Sarah turned to look at me.

"She thinks the draft I sent is too sad," I continued. "And has too much about Down syndrome in it."

"Hah!" Sarah laughed. "Told you."

"Yes, you did. And I flew all the way up to New York, and she said the same thing you did, right here in Durham."

Sarah laughed again, and smacked her thigh with her palm. Chuckled.

"I need to come up with some happy stories," I said.

Sarah turned and nodded. It had been self-evident.

"Can you help me think of some?" I asked.

"Not really," she said. "You were always working. Mom was always stressed."

"But I need some happy stories," I said.

"Good luck with that, Dad."

———

On movie nights, Sarah's favorite place to eat was Chick-fil-A, because they had gluten-free choices, and she had celiac disease. She always got grilled chicken without the bun. This time she decided to get the carrot and raisin salad to go with it, instead of fries, so she could get nachos and cheese at the movie.

"I don't want to eat too much," Sarah said, "so I don't vomit." A year previously, Sarah had upchucked into her lap while at the movies with Gin Wiegand, a friend of the family. Gin is Sarah's other movie buddy. Sarah will call her and say, "Gin, let's go see *The King's Speech*," or "Gin, wanna go see *Toy Story 3*?" They also ride together when Gin's delivering meals-on-wheels.

"Make sure you cut the chicken up into small pieces," I said. "And chew a lot."

"Yeah," she said. "So I don't choke."

I nodded.

"When I choked on that giant jawbreaker, everyone was freaking out." Holding her fork in her fist, she held the meat down and began to saw across it with the plastic knife.

"Jawbreaker?" I hadn't heard about this time.

"At home," she said. "The staff, the other residents, everyone was going nuts."

"It's scary," I said. When she's choking, Sarah's eyes open wide, and her chest and abdomen heave. She sits, lurching, her mouth open, silent, tears streaming down her face. Once it's out, she goes back to eating as if nothing happened.

She nodded, and cut her meat into smaller pieces. "Well, your book is going to scare the parents of children with Down syndrome," she said.

"You think?"

"All that stuff about Hitler killing people with special needs?" Sarah took a bite, chewed, and swallowed. "They're going to be saying, 'Oh my God, what if he comes back to life!!! He's going to kill my baby!!!'" She then laughed at how ridiculous that would be.

"But it's history people need to know," I said.

"Maybe."

———

"What was the guy's name who said people with Down syndrome couldn't think about symbols?" Sarah and I were sitting in the plush seats of the theater, waiting for the movie to start.

"Say again?"

"The guy in your book. The one who said people with disabilities were animals."

"Oh," I said. "John Locke. But he didn't say that people with disabilities were animals. He just said that beasts couldn't form abstract thoughts, and that neither could people with intellectual disabilities."

"I still don't like him." Sarah's tray of corn chips and cheese was perched on her lap, untouched.

"I like a lot of what he wrote," I said. "But he was wrong about that."

"Well," Sarah said. She shifted in her seat, and looked at me. "Are you going to leave him in your book?"

"I'm not sure," I said. "I'm still working on it."

"Well, yeah," Sarah said. "And what about the parents of children with Down syndrome? What are they going to say when they read your book?"

"I don't know, Sarah. Mostly I hope they see how great you are."

"Nice try, Dad." She laughed.

"I'm serious."

She shrugged. "I still don't like that Locke guy."

———

John's twenty-first birthday landed on Mother's Day. He had run into some problems in college and was back home, working a maintenance job: cleaning the pool, painting fences, and sweeping the tennis courts at the Duke Faculty Club.

Mother's Day had always been a difficult time for Sally. Cards and flowers and breakfast in bed—all the things husbands and children think we're supposed to do—seemed to touch a sadness that always stayed beneath the surface.

Sarah had called Sally a couple of weeks previously, suggesting that they go to a movie together to celebrate Mother's Day—a romantic comedy. Just the girls. Sally picked her up at the group home, and they went to a matinee showing of a movie based on a book by Nicholas Sparks, *The Lucky One*. Then they came back to the house.

I'd ordered pizza, per John's request, and had made one for Sarah with a gluten-free crust Sally had picked up at Whole Foods. We ate in the dining room. Sally and I brought in the twelve-inch chocolate chip cookie, twenty-one tiny flames wavering at the periphery. After the "Happy Birthday" song, John blew out the candles.

He opened his presents: a couple of nice shirts from Sally and me. Half a dozen socks. A card from Sarah. We then went into the computer room for a slideshow I'd put together. Baby pictures, John as a toddler. "Endless Summer" playing in the background, the guitar music seamlessly matching each image as it came up. A green-eyed four-year-old in a red plastic fireman's hat. John's arms up in the air, grass-surfing down a small hill in the yard. John on the rope swing, the thick yellow rope's end whipping the air, John's grip tight. John and Sam running through the sprinkler. Stilts, bicycles, the boys lying on their backs on the roof of the playhouse. John standing straight in a blue and yellow Cub Scout uniform. A sleepy middle school kid in a sleeping bag. Skim-boarding at the beach, body curving graceful as a wave. Family pictures—frowns and smiles and mugging. Cousins and aunts and uncles, and grandparents. John and Sam wearing sunglasses on the Golden Gate Bridge. Graduation day, purple robe and mortarboard. Guitar music in the background.

The slideshow ended with a photograph of the plaster casts of their hands that we'd made at the beach when Sarah was ten, John six, and Sam four. The surfaces were textured with sand and tiny bits of seashell. Their palms faced outward, each one distinct: Sam's hand so small, John's slightly larger, fingers splayed as if stopped mid-wave, Sarah's fingers curved ever so slightly, as if gently cupping the air.

The last image dissolved and the music faded. We all gave subtle nods.

"Thanks," John said, still facing the computer's monitor. He'd wiped his eye a few times with the back of his index finger.

"That was good." Sam gave a short nod.

Sally patted my shoulder.

"It was touching," Sarah said.

Sarah went out to the front porch to swing some more before she went back to the group home. She'd forgotten her music player, so she didn't sing—she just made her impossibly high arcs over and over.

Sally and I put the leftover pizza in the fridge, cleared the plates.

"I can take her back," I said.

Sally nodded. "Thanks."

"Can I take the Mustang?"

She tossed me the keys. I no longer had my luxury automobile: there had been a credit card I couldn't pay down, and I felt silly driving a car with leather seats while I owed money on consumer debt. So I sold the car and paid off the Visa.

I still had the pickup I'd bought before John was born, but it wasn't nearly as much fun to drive as Sally's Mustang, with its five-speed manual transmission, convertible top, and Sirius XM radio.

Sarah and I settled into the Mustang, and rumbled down the street. A chorus from a Broadway show came from the quadraphonic speakers. I stopped at the corner and clicked the search button until I found the E Street Band in the middle of *Darkness on the Edge of Town*.

"Mom and I listen to show tunes," Sarah said.

"Yeah, but you and I listen to The Boss."

"Not really."

"You don't like Bruce Springsteen?"

"No."

"Show tunes?"

She nodded.

I pushed a preselect button. Hits from the sixties. Another button. Hits from the seventies.

Sarah leaned forward, pushed a button, and settled back into her seat. A show tune cascaded from the speaker, conjuring slender men in top hats and long-legged showgirls twirling canes and top hats.

I looked over at her. *Really?*

She raised her eyebrows. "What?"

"Nothing." I settled into the bucket seat and pulled into traffic.

"Can you come to an open house on Wednesday?" Sarah asked. "For Voices Together." The choir Sarah sang in. "You could put it in your book."

"I'd love to," I said, "but I'm going to be working a string of night shifts. Four in a row."

"Ouch."

We drove.

"It's coming along," I said.

Sarah said something I couldn't understand.

"Say again?"

"The happy stuff," she said. "About Down syndrome."

I looked at her, and then back to the road.

"The good things about it," she continued.

I kept driving.

"You could write about how people with Down syndrome are more sensitive," she said, gesturing with her palm up. "Like the girl in *Glee*."

"Well," I said. "There you go."

"And people with Down syndrome are kinder, and better listeners," she said. "Smarter, too."

"I guess I could put it in."

"It would make it a better book," she said.

I nodded. We drove.

She looked over at me. "I just don't see what's so bad about Down syndrome."

The parents and professionals who came before us changed the way the world thinks about people with disabilities. Sarah, and our entire family, has benefited from those changes. But the change that really had to happen wasn't in the world. It was in me.

Over time, and as I wrote this book, Sarah became less and less "my daughter with Down syndrome" and more and more "my daughter."

No qualifiers needed.

EPILOGUE

Sally cried for our daughter on the day she was born, but it would be twenty-two years before I cried like that. It happened while I was still working on this book, before I ever showed it to Sarah.

I was at a writers' conference, in a workshop led by a teacher I had long admired. He assigned an exercise in which we cut our manuscript into chunks of text—actual paper and scissors—and rearranged them. The empty spaces were supposed to open up our minds. At first, it seemed precious, gimmicky. But my teacher's writing was so incisive and clear, I decided to give it a try, see if it worked.

We were at the Atlantic Center for the Arts in New Smyrna Beach, Florida. About two miles inland, the Center was a small cluster of buildings, all redwood siding and angled rooflines jutting into the sky. The buildings seemed to float in a marshy sea of plant life—the spiky fans of palmetto palms, wild magnolias, scrub oaks, and Spanish moss. The illusion was enhanced by the weathered wooden walkways between buildings. Without the waist-high railings one might expect, they looked like piers, jutting into the lush green foliage.

Our workshop met in a small and narrow library, with two walls of books and two walls of windows. For this exercise our teacher had arranged for us to use one of the artist's studios. It was a large open room with a concrete floor, natural light, and five long worktables with paint-splattered surfaces that gave the place a Jackson Pollock feel.

I started out calmly enough, laying out two rows of blank typing paper, stark and white against the reds and blues and yellows of my workspace. I glanced around, and my classmates were all busy cutting and taping. I enjoyed the arts-and-crafts feel of the activity, the absorption of scissors and tape.

I cut several paragraphs free and spread them out onto the pages. They looked like chunky fortune cookie slips. So much white space and so few words. I glanced at my classmates' work. They all had more pieces of text, and they were all busy moving the pieces around, rearranging them. My pages looked bare. I turned to the teacher, who was pinning pieces of a poem onto a wall. "Can we use pictures?"

He turned. "Sure. Whatever helps." He went back to his work.

I walked to the computer center and printed off pictures of things I'd been writing about. Three portraits of John

Langdon Down, the "father of Down syndrome." He was wearing a frock coat and a black bow tie. Two photographs of Jérôme Lejeune, the scientist credited with discovering the extra 21st chromosome that causes Down syndrome.

I printed out the karyotype that Sarah's geneticist gave me after she was born. It was an eight-by-ten photograph of her chromosomes all lined up two by two, except for the 21st chromosome—it had three. I printed a snapshot of Sarah dressed up as a wicked princess for Halloween. Another photograph of Sarah, twenty-two years old, in the group home. She was sitting between the two framed movie posters—one with Gene Kelly, Debbie Reynolds, and Donald O'Connor skipping forward in yellow slickers, umbrellas twirling: *Singing in the Rain*. In the other, Audrey Hepburn posed in a slinky black dress, neck encircled with diamonds and a tabby cat, black gloves up past the elbows: *Breakfast at Tiffany's*.

I placed these pictures on the nearly-blank pages, and stepped back from the table and stared at the pages, trying to let the process work. I leaned forward to jot a note to myself in blue ink on the white page, and then stared some more.

The picture of Sarah's chromosomes entirely filled the page. I leaned down and wrote, "This picture looks so big. So real." I looked over at a snapshot of Sarah. It looked so small there, askew in the corner of an empty page. It hit me that from the day she was born, I'd seen a diagnosis instead of a daughter. This struck me like a bolt of lightning splitting a tree. I felt as if something in my chest had been riven—my aorta torn away from my heart, or my trachea ripped free from my lungs. I did not know my daughter.

I felt tears coming, so I left, pushing through the door of the studio and out into the sun. I made it partway down the unrailed walkway. But this feeling in my chest was too big to control. I jumped down into the bushes, pushing alongside a building, the branches scratching my face, vines catching my feet. I came to a deck, a bare platform without railings, waist-high, jutting into the thicket. I stopped and wailed. I was undone. Unhinged. Bereft. I heard my howls rushing out from my body and into the air. The keening finally slowed to sobs. I became aware again of the sand under my feet. I took a gulp of air. The breeze was soft against my face. The trees swayed gently.

"Are you okay?" I heard someone call from the walkway, a disembodied voice coming through the tangle of plants.

"Yes," I answered. I took a deep breath. "I'm fine."

"You sure?"

"Yes," I said. "Thanks." I held my breath and stood motionless. I didn't want anyone to see me.

I heard a few footsteps on the wooden pier, and then a door in the building I was standing next to open, and then close. Fuck. I'd been wailing right outside someone's work-shop.

I blew my nose on my fingers and slung the snot into the bushes. I wiped my fingers on the cuffs of my jeans, and wiped my face with my shirtsleeve. I felt empty inside. Clean.

I pushed through the bushes back to the walkway. No one was there. Good. I climbed up onto the walkway and found a bathroom, where I splashed my face and dried it.

The studio was empty: they must have gone back to the library. At my table, I stared at the photograph of Sarah and gently straightened it on its page, glad that it wasn't too late. My daughter would forgive me. It's the way she was.

When Sarah was four days old and a friend told me that I would learn about patience, acceptance, and unconditional love, I'd taken this to mean that I would develop these traits by necessity, through raising a daughter with special needs. Turns outs I learned about them by observing them in my daughter.

I walked back to the library, where the group sat around the table. The teacher looked up. "Thought we'd lost you," he said. "Did you go to make more copies?"

"No," I said, gesturing outside. "I was needing to cry."

He looked at me and nodded, as if to say, "That some-times happens."

I felt calm and expectant, like that glittering moment right after a summer thunderstorm. I'd been given a second chance.

———

At lunch, our teacher walked up with his plate and silverware. "Can I join you?"

"Please."

"The other workshop heard you."

I winced. "Sorry."

He waved it away. "They thought it was an animal caught in a trap."

"Not far off," I said.

"You're in the middle of it." He took my shoulder and gently shook it. He smiled. I felt as if he was welcoming me into a new place. A place I needed to be.

"Yup," I said, using Sarah's shorthand way of summing up a complicated truth. I was eager to get back home, and see my daughter, and get to know her.

ACKNOWLEDGMENTS

Beautiful Eyes would not have been possible without Sarah. I will always be grateful for the honesty of her response to this book, and her gracious acceptance of the ways in which it has failed to capture her depth, courage, wisdom, and humor.

This book was, at times, painful to write. Sally has been steadfastly supportive. Without her encouragement I doubt that I could have completed it. Sally also helped me remember and understand what really happened in the early years of our marriage and family. She was honest when she thought I wasn't remembering it correctly, or rendering it accurately. John and Sam have both read it, and offered invaluable insights.

So many other people helped me as I wrote this book; it is inevitable that I will fail to mention someone, and I wince at that thought. But here goes. The people at the London Metropolitan Archives, and The John Langdon Down Centre were very generous with their time and expertise, as were the people at the Hartheim Memorial.

Judy Goldman, Peggy Payne, Nick Flynn, and Mary Akers all offered invaluable help with the writing itself. So did Sally. Michelle Tessler is the best agent I could hope for. Allegra Huston's herculean efforts improved the formatting, style, and accuracy of the book. Rebecca Schultz and Angie Shih helped shepherd the book along at Norton, and the design team has created a beautiful book. I love the cover.

I don't know how Jill Bialosky does what she does, but she helped me see what the book could be. I'm a better writer for it, and this book's a better book.

NOTES

1. Stanley M. Gartier, "The chromosome number in humans: a brief history." *Nature Reviews Genetics* 7, 655–60 (August 2006): doi:10.1038/nrg1917.
2. Peter S. Harper, *A Short History of Medical Genetics* (Oxford and New York: Oxford University Press, 2008), 143–45.
3. Other researchers of the time studied human spermatogonial cells, and cytologists "literally waited at the foot of the gallows in order to fix the testis on an executed criminal immediately after death before the chromosomes would clump." M. J. Kottler, "From 48 to 46: cytological technique, preconception, and the counting of the human chromosomes," *Bulletin of the History of Medicine*, 1974, available at: ncbi.nlm.nih.gov.
4. Wolfgang Saxon, "Joe Hin Tjio, 82: Research Biologist Counted Chromosomes," *New York Times*, December 7, 2001.
5. Jérôme Lejeune, Marthe Gautier, and Raymond Turpin, "Étude des Chromosomes Somatiques de Neuf Enfants Mongoliens," *Comptes rendus des séances de l'Académie des Sciences* 248: 1721–959. A translated version appeared in *Papers on Human Genetics*, edited by Samuel H. Boyer (New York: Prentice Hall, 1963), 238–40.
6. Daniel J. Kevles, "Mongolian Imbecility," in *Mental Retardation in America: A Historical Perspective*, edited by Steven Noll and James W. Trent, Jr. (New York and London: New York University Press, 2004) 123–27.
7. BBC News: http://news.bbc.co.uk/2/hi/7967173.stm.
8. Clara Lejeune, *Life is a Blessing: A Biography of Jérôme Lejeune* (San Francisco: Ignatius Press, 2000). Translated from the original French edition: *La Vie est un monheur: Jerome Lejeune, mon père* (Paris: Criterion, 1997); Frederick Hecht, "Jérôme Lejeune (1926–94): In Memoriam," *Am. J. Hum. Gent.* 55 (1994): 201–2.
9. S. Gilgenkrantz and E. M. Rivera, "The history of cytogenet-

ics: Portraits of some pioneers," *Annales de génétique* 46, no. 4 (October–December 2003): 433–42.

10. Marthe Gautier and Peter Harper, "Fiftieth anniversary of trisomy 21: returning to a discovery," *Human Genetics* 126 (2009): 317–24.

11. Ibid.; Gilgenkrantz and Rivera, "The history of cytogenetics," 433–42.

12. Gautier and Harper, "Fiftieth anniversary of trisomy 21," 317–24.

13. "Perhaps no man ever had a more judicious or more methodical genius, or was a more acute logician than Mr. Locke . . ." Available at: http://www.class.uidaho.edu/mickelsen/texts/voltaire_on_locke.htm.

14. C. F. Goodey, "John Locke's idiots in the natural history of the mind," *History of Psychiatry* 5, no. 18, pt. 2 (June 1994): 215–50.

15. John Locke, *An Essay Concerning Human Understanding*, Book 4, ch. 4, section 16.

16. David Livingstone Smith, *Less than Human: Why We Demean, Enslave, and Exterminate Others* (New York: St Martin's Press, 2011).

17. Josef Warkany, "Congenital Malformations in the Past," *Journal of Chronic Diseases*, August 1959, 84–97.

18. Júlio César Pangas, "Historical Review: Birth Malformations in Babylon and Assyria," *American Journal of Medical Genetics* 91 (2000): 318–21; Kathryn L. Moseley, "The History of Infanticide in Western Society," *Issues in Law and Medicine* 1, no. 5 (1986).

19. Moseley, "The History of Infanticide in Western Society."

20. Phillip Lopate, *The Art of the Personal Essay: An Anthology from the Classical Era to the Present*, (New York: Anchor Books/Doubleday, 1994).

21. Michel de Montaigne, *The Complete Essays of Montaigne*, translated by Donald Frame (Palo Alto, CA: Stanford University Press, 1958), 538.

22. Warkany, "Congenital Malformations in the Past."

23. Ibid.

24. E. Martin, *Histoire des monstres de l'antiquité jusqu'à nos jours* (Paris: Reinwald et Cie., 1880).

25. http://www.cbsnews.com/8301-503544_162-6232759-503544.html; "Del. Marshall says abortion remark misconstrued, apologizes," Fredrick Kunkle, *Washington Post*, February 23, 2010.

26. http://www.anencephalie-info.org/e/index.php.

27. Dale Evans, *Angel Unaware* (Grand Rapids, MI: Fleming H. Revell, 1953).

28. Cheryl Rogers-Barnett and Frank Thompson, *Cowboy Princess: Life*

With My Parents Roy Rogers and Dale Evans (Lanham, MD: Taylor Trade Publishing, 2003).

29. H. Allen Smith, "King of the Cowboys," *Life* 15, no. 2 (July 12, 1943): 47–52.
30. Susan Schweik, *The Ugly Laws: Disability in Public* (New York and London: New York University Press, 2009).
31. Lorraine Wilgosh, Dick Sobsey, and Kate Scorgie, "Cultural Constructions of Families of Children with Disabilities," in *Culture Plus the State,* edited by James Gifford and Gabrielle Zezulka-Mailloux (Edmonton: University of Alberta Press, CRC Studio, 2003).
32. Hilary Spurling, *Pearl Buck in China: Journey to the Good Earth* (New York: Simon and Schuster, 2010).
33. Pearl S. Buck, "The Child Who Never Grew," *Ladies' Home Journal,* May 1950.
34. "Legalize Mercy Killings," *Collier's Magazine,* May 20, 1939. Details on contributors available at: http://colliersmagazine.com/.
35. Foster Kennedy, "The Problem of Social Control of the Congenital Defective: Education, Sterilization, Euthanasia," *American Journal of Psychiatry* 99 (1942): 13–16; Thorsten Noack and Heiner Fangerau, "Eugenics, Euthanasia, and Aftermath," *International Journal of Mental Health* 36, no. 1 (Spring 2007): 112–24; M. Louis Offen, "Dealing with 'Defectives,'" *Neurology* 61, no. 5 (September 9, 2003): 668–73.
36. Pearl S. Buck, *The Child Who Never Grew* (New York: John Day, 1950).
37. Roy Rogers and Dale Evans, with Jane and Michael Stern, *Happy Trails: Our Life Story* (New York: Simon and Schuster, 1994).
38. Andrew S. Levitas and Cheryl S. Reid, "Historical Review: An Angel With Down Syndrome in a Sixteenth-Century Flemish Nativity Painting," *American Journal of Medical Genetics* part A, vol. 116A, issue 4 (February 1, 2003): 399–405.
39. Susie Nash, *Oxford History of Art: Northern Renaissance Art* (New York: Oxford University Press, 2008).
40. Maryan W. Ainsworth, *From Van Eyck to Bruegel: Early Netherlandish Painting in the Metropolitan Museum of Art* (New York: Metropolitan Museum of Art, 1999).
41. Guy C. Bauman, *The Jack and Belle Linsky Collection in the Metropolitan Museum of Art* (New York: Metropolitan Museum of Art, 1984), 68.

42. Max J. Friedländer, *Early Netherlandish Painting From Van Eyck to Bruegel* (London: Phaidon Press, 1965), 34.

43. Herbert Hohler, "Changes in Facial Expression as a Result of Plastic Surgery in Mongoloid Children." *Aesthetic Plastic Surgery* 1, no. 1 (December 1976): 245–50. Dr. Hohler was awarded the Heinrich-Bechhold Medal 1977 for this paper.

44. Amy Harmon, "The DNA Age: Prenatal Test Puts Down Syndrome In Hard Focus," *New York Times*, May 9, 2007.

45. Eunice Kennedy Shriver, "Prenatal Testing: Supporting parents of children with Down syndrome," *America: The National Catholic Weekly* 196, no. 17 (May 14, 2007).

46. Roger D. Klein, MD, JD, and Maurice J. Mahone, MD, JD, "Medical Legal Issues in Prenatal Diagnosis," *Clinics in Perinatology*, part I, vol. 34, issue 2 (June 2007): 287–97.

47. Friedlander, *Early Netherlandish Painting*, 39–43.

48. Gregory Gallagher, *By Trust Betrayed* (New York: Henry Holt, 1990), 195.

49. http://www.charlotteobserver.com/2011/08/24/2550278/speaker-wants-to-compensate-sterilized.html.

50. John Langdon Down, "Mental Affections of Childhood and Youth" (lecture). Published in *Classics in Developmental Medicine*, vol. 5 (Oxford: Blackwell Scientific Publications, 1990), 3–4.

51. John Langdon Down, "Observations on the Ethnic Classification of Idiots," London Hospital Clinical Report 3 (1866): 259–62.

52. http://www.princeton.edu/~psinger/faq.html, accessed May 29, 2012.

53. Helga Kuhse, ed. *Unsanctifying Human Life: Essays on Ethics* (New York: Blackwell, 2002), 2; Michael Specter, "The Dangerous Philosopher," *The New Yorker*, September 6, 1999.

54. Arthur Caplan, *Time*, April 18, 2005.

55. Peter Singer, *Practical Ethics* (Cambridge, UK: Cambridge University Press, 1979).

56. James Boswell, *Life of Johnson* (Oxford: Oxford University Press, 2008), 333.

57. I learned this during a visit to the Harthiem Castle Memorial, a T-4 killing center, in Alkoven, Austria.

58. Harriet McBryde Johnson, "Unspeakable Conversations," *New York Times Magazine*, February 16, 2003.